INITIATION *into*

NUMEROLOGY

INITIATION *into* NUMEROLOGY

A Practical Guide for Reading Your Own Numbers

JOHANN HEYSS

WEISER BOOKS

York Beach, Maine, USA

First published in 2001 by
Weiser Books
P. O. Box 612
York Beach, ME 03910-0612
www.weiserbooks.com

Library of Congress Cataloging-in-Publication Data
Heyss, Johann.
    [Iniciação à numerologia. English]
    Initiation into numerology : a practical guide for reading your own
    numbers / Johann Heyss.
       p. cm.
    Includes bibliographical references and index.
    ISBN 1-57863-194-7 (pbk. : alk. paper)
      1. Numerology. I. Title.
  BF1623.P9 H4313 2001
  133.3'35—dc21   00–068528

VG
Typeset in 10/12 Palatino

Cover design by Kathryn Sky-Peck

Printed in the United States of America

08 07 06 05 04 03 02 01
8 7 6 5 4 3 2 1

*For all the people who have helped me
with the research of numbers and magick*

CONTENTS

List of Figures and Tables..............................8

Author's Note 9

PART 0

On Numbers 11

PART I

What Is Numerology?.....................................15

PART II

The Numbers.................................25

PART III

The Chart 63

Bibliography 117

Index 121

About the Author...........................125

Figures

Figure 1. Yin, yang and neutral positions 19
Figure 2. The spiral projection of numbers 23
Figure 3. Letter and number equivalents 24
Figure 4. The tetractys 30
Figure 5. The extremeties of essential numbers 48
Figure 6. The name graphic 76
Figure 7. John Lennon's name graphic 77

Tables

Table 1. Lennon's Dharma Number 73
Table 2. Lennon's Karma Number 74
Table 3. Numbers and Professions 80
Table 4. Numbers and Sex 82
Table 5. Determining Lennon's Personal Year 86
Table 6. Lennon's 2nd Cycle Ends 88
Table 7. Numbers and the Major Arcana in the Thoth Deck . .93
Table 8. Numbers and the Minor Arcana in the Thoth Deck . .95
Table 9. John Winston Lennon's Life Path 99
Table 10. The Meaning of Letters in the Life Graph 104
Table 11. Numerological Conjunctions 106
Table 12. Personal Years and Months .112

AUTHOR'S NOTE

I do not think that destiny is fully predictable, nor that your name can be good *or* bad, or that you can bring more luck into your life by changing your name. I am a skeptical person, so this book is the result of eleven years of research. The method of numerology that I present in this book is very objective—yet subtle—ready to be used every day, not as theory, but as a practical technique to help you see the bigger picture.

—Johann Heyss
New York City

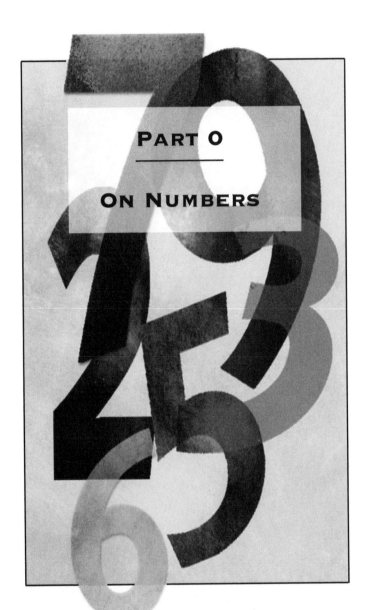

PART 0

ON NUMBERS

On Numbers

As with the tarot, we start our study with "0." Therefore to begin the study of numbers, we now start with "Part 0." To become a profound reader of numbers, you must learn the numbers; that is, you should understand them from a new point of view, which is not the strictly mathematical sense—even though you will note that all the assumptions about the personality of numbers are based on their mathematical qualities. Throughout this book, you'll be learning different nuances of number symbolism. In this section, you'll learn the basic numbers 0–9 and the master numbers 11 and 22.

The following list provides an introduction to the principal numbers, giving you the basis for understanding the combinations that form the composed numbers.

0

Nothingness, emptiness, the occult, the hidden, pre-existence, absence, abstractness.

1

Maleness, existence, affirmation, power, strength, activity, clarity, independence, movement.

2

Femaleness, continuation, delicacy, intuition, subjectivity, darkness, dependence, quietness.

3

Child, manifestation, creativity, expression, communication, agility, colors, happiness, inconstancy.

4

Work, concretizing, constancy, dedication, routine, patience, honesty, limitation, discipline.

5

Changes, transformation, travels, sexuality, superficiality, curiosity, the rebel, a sense of adventure.

6

Family, multiplication, hometown, love, affection, conformity, acceptance, tranquility, creative talent.

7

Introspection, meditation, isolation, intellect, study, philosophy, solitude, wisdom.

8

Materialism, improvement, justice, pragmatism, rationalism, ambition, establishment, society.

9

Community, breakthrough, rupture, advancement, the globe, anxiety, rush, message, energy, confusion, charity, will.

11

Iconoclasm, transcendence, exception, difference, anticipation, prophecy, genius, misplaced, enhancing, magic, initiation.

22

Attainment, finalization, magnitude, spirituality, weight, contrast, canonization, enlightenment.

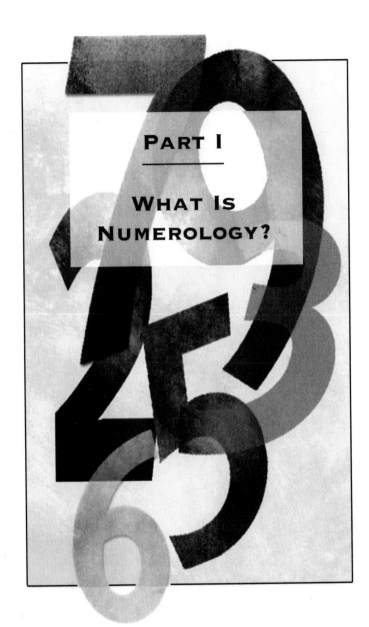

PART I

WHAT IS NUMEROLOGY?

What Numerology Is

In order to define numerology, we must first define numbers. Numbers are representations of quantity, and quantity relates to duality or polarity, which is found in every reality. Everything is dual: day and night, good and evil, man and woman, etc. So is the objective world that we deal with every day. When unity—which is God, the Soul-Mother, or any term you prefer—was divided, it gave birth to duality. Multiplicity also comes from duality. Through multiplicity one can understand duality, as through duality one can assimilate unity. Numerology is a subjective system that can show us another level of interpretation in the matters of life.

The best known researcher of numbers was Pythagoras, but we should not confuse his studies of metaphysical mathematics with numerology. Numerology is based on his concept of numbers as a metaphysical power, a parallel world that rises through our world's little details—the actual essence of the universe. Let us say that Pythagoras seemed, according to the teachings his pupils propagated, to be unconcerned about this kind of analysis. Pythagoras influenced several philosophers, and this is how we know about his philosophy, since he did not write books.

One of the ways that leads to the comprehension of the world is by attempting to understand people—not necessarily to agree with them, nor to explain them, but to grasp their nature. The numerological chart is a powerful tool for that purpose. It is simple yet deep. The only data required for the composition of the chart is your complete original name and your date of birth. These data will be the basis for the calculations. Don't be afraid of complicated calculations. I can assure you that your knowedge of mathematics is probably much better than mine! Each number combination reflects a certain aspect of your personality and shows an archetypal energy that is the root of the personality.

Each number has a "behavior" in mathematics; that is, each number has its own characteristics (for example, some are even, others are odd; some are multiples of three; some can be divided by others, but cannot produce an exact operation with others, and so on). So if you think by analogy, those characteristics will reflect (not induce) behaviors and situations in your life, according to the translation from the "language of numbers" to "human language," no matter what language you speak. The numerological chart is a puzzle in which each little piece has an individual meaning, even though this meaning is fully comprehensible only by comparing contraries.

Your name reflects your *self* in the chart, while the date of birth reveals *how* this self lives. This is easy to understand: your complete original name actually works as a kind of label. Therefore, the investigation of the symbolism of that name will unveil the so-called owner of the name.

Similarly, the date of birth symbolizes the start of the journey, and how the rest of it will be affected. Note that this data *does not* symbolize a fixed destiny, for there is always an unknown element in life, and we should not overlook it. On the other hand, by knowing the numbers we are also able to observe a soul in the same way we observe a face in a picture.

The first numerical distinction we can make is between the positive/masculine and the negative/feminine groups. It does not imply anything concerning better or worse, or sexuality. It only implies polarity, being that odd numbers are always virile and aggressive in different ways, while even ones carry some subtlety and delicacy. Also, when we add an odd and even number, the result will always be odd, in the same way that two even numbers added together will produce another even number. It shows clearly how demanding the odd numbers are, always imposing themselves upon the even; and how defensive the even numbers can be, protecting their similar in a circle.

Let's start with the elementary numbers: 1, 2, 3, 4, 5, 6, 7, 8, 9. These cannot be reduced; they represent essential archetypes, the basic manifestation of personality or a situation. All the other numbers (except 11 and 22, for reasons we will learn later) can be reduced like this. For example: 18 = 1 + 8 = 9. This is a simplification of a method created by Pythagoras in order to understand the essence of a number.

The master numbers are 11 and 22. We cannot reduce these numbers because they represent the exceptions to every rule, so they are linked to distinctive people and situations.

The result of any operation is enhanced by the observation of where the number is placed. If we make a triangular combination (see figure 1, below) of positive, negative, and neutral numbers, we have a yang position—which means that the one at your left (on the triangle's right), is its positive side. The yin position is on your right side (the triangle's left), and the lower extremity of the triangle will be the neutral one, or the combination of both aspects. If an odd number is placed at the yin position (a feminine position), the combination is actually different from the same number if it were placed in a yang position. For example, consider 29/11: the soft number 2 occupies a strong first position, and the active number 9 lies on the position of calmness. This is the source of the androgyny of 11. If you draw a triangle and try placing some numbers on it, you might see how these numbers work.

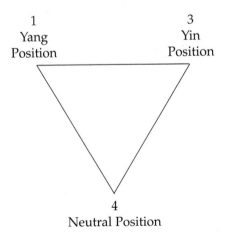

Figure 1. Yang, yin, and neutral positions.

The yang position contains 1, the first of the male numbers. The number 1 represents the ruling polarity, the basis of all numbers. The number 1 gives the qualities of pulse, leadership, and dynamism to any number. The number 3 is an odd number placed in a subtle polarity. Being the number of communication, translating both vibrations can be successful, so 3 works as a bridge linking the impulse of 1 through 3 which moves toward 4. This needs some kind of filtration, for 1 is not fully harmonized with 4, and 3 provides this kind of communication. So, the 4 that comes from 13, is influenced by its "father" 1, and its "mother" 3, and the natural low-profile that is expected of 4 is affected by the energy of its "parents." This kind of a 4 is the most creative of all the other uses of number 4 (31, 40, etc.). If we consider 31, we may first note that 1 occupies the passive position of the triangle, and 1 doesn't work properly as a conductor in a passive way because of its imperative essence. In terms of initiation, 31, on the other hand, is a very important number, but it is also one that represents an obstacle you must overcome before experiencing enlightenment. Dealing with this obstacle defines your life, for better or for worse.

We must keep in mind that a composed number is the root that influences the basic number. The composed numbers are the father and mother from which the basic number inherits its particular characteristics. For example, 6 is always a 6, but depending on the numbers that compose it, some characteristics are stronger than others. A 6 that is composed from 15 is always more passionate, strong, and less quiet—characteristics of the "father" 1 and the "mother" 5 that make 6 tend toward the violent side of passion. A 6 that comes from 24 is the weakest one, for the yin aspects of 6 are reinforced by 2 and 4, resulting in a 6 that is weakened by a lack of yang energy. The number 33, a "special" 6, indicates, as do the master numbers, either enlightenment or mental illness (note that 33 is not a master number, but does exhibit the same double current of energy found in master numbers).

The basic number is the archetype, and the composed number shows the tendencies of the archetype. The following list will give you some brief examples of how composed numbers influence basic numbers:

1 is the leader, but number 10 tends toward a paternal style in leadership, 19 toward an authoritarian style, and 28 toward perfectionism in leadership;

2 is the cooperator, but 20 tends to cooperate on a higher, spiritual level;

3 is the communicator, but 12 has difficulty in speaking its mind, 21 struggles with anxiety in expressing itself, while 30 communicates without angst;

4 is the organizer, but 13 tends to exceed the rules, while 31 makes the rules;

5 is the rebel, but 14 tends to repress 5's rebellious predisposition, 23 tends toward inflammatory words and actions, and 32 finds balance through liberty;

6 is emotion, 15 tends toward strong feelings, 24 toward weak emotions, and 33 lies between the extremes;

7 is the intellect, but 16 tends toward destruction while 25 tends toward construction;

8 is material circumstances and concerns, 17 is inclined to be hopeful in thought and behavior, while 26 tends toward fragility and pessimism;

9 is freedom and motion, but 18 tends to avoid paths that lead to intense emotions. 27 usually searches the inner world and 36 the outer world;

11 is the yang aspect of spirituality, but 29 approaches it in a more "conventional" way, and 38 in a more "material" way;

22 is the yin aspect of spirituality, and its composed numbers are all over 100, which makes the influences more complex and better left to a more advanced study.

If you don't pay attention to the process of the formation of a number (which is shown in composed—not reduced—numbers), you can't really say you understand the symbol and how it works. For example, water is always water, but it can be filtered or nonfiltered, sea water, muddy water, river water, distilled water, ice—all water, yet all different kinds of H^2O.

You can also assimilate what a number means if you pay attention to its mathematical behavior, whether it is divisible or not, and with which numbers and circumstances, etc. In addition, the analyses of the spiral projection of numbers (see figure 2), explains a lot about their relationships, behavior, and personality.

The first step of the spiral contains the elementary numbers, the basic patterns, that breed all the other existing numerical combinations. This is step zero. The second step of the spiral is inhabited by number 1 and its generation; that is, number 1, itself, in combination with all the other basic patterns and elementary numbers, including the combination of 1 and 1 (11). Therefore, all composed numbers beginning with 1 are supposed to have a clear influence on the meaning of the whole of the number. In addition, the first number in that level is 10, which we can reduce to 1, as well as the last number in line, 19, which can also be turned into 1.

So the same happens in the next step, the one for number 2 and so on until number 9. (Note that 11 is the result of 29, but we are not supposed to reduce it. Still, it is a kind of "substitution" for 2, and, in a sense, its natural development.) That is so because in this present study we will concentrate in the first thirty-three numbers, for they are the most essential qabalistic archetypes, the ones representing the path and the evolution of all beings.

We can only understand the combinations if we have previously understood the essential meaning of the elementary numbers. We have already had a brief presentation of these numbers in Part O of this book, but that was just a spark, a twilight that will be clarified in the next chapter.

Before we can move on, we must understand the basic correlation between numbers and letters shown in figure 3.

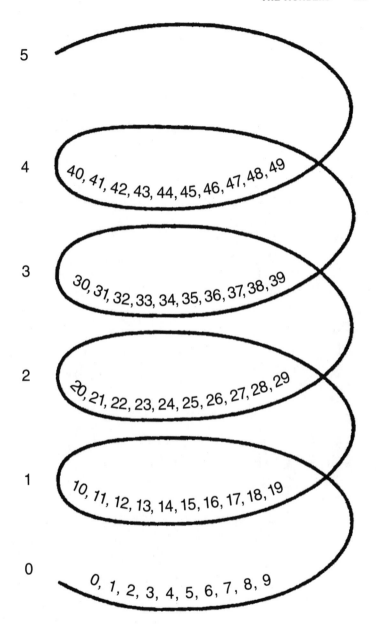

Figure 2. The spiral projection of numbers.

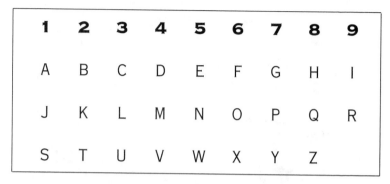

Figure 3. Letter and number equivalents.

When you calculate a numerological chart, you will turn the letters of the name into numbers. The logic of this association comes from the idea that the same energy, or principle, appears in different worlds: the same principle for A should be **1**, because they're both the first of their systems. Verily, the Sun is the first—the leader of the solar system, so the Sun or "A" is number 1, and so on. In ancient times, there was no difference between chemistry and alchemy, astronomy and astrology, mathematics and numerology, sacred and profane, and in the same way, there was no difference between letters and numbers. That's why the Hebrew and Greek alphabets are composed of letters that happen to also be numbers. So numerology would be kind of a Qabalah for modern times, no matter how strange that may sound.

Again, we concentrate on the elementary numbers when we attribute numerical values to letters. But don't forget that *A, J,* and *S* are all different forms of number 1. And there is a difference between 1, 10 and 19. That's why *A* is more shiny, *J* is the most subtle, and *S* is the strongest—all forms of 1 in their similarities and contrasts.

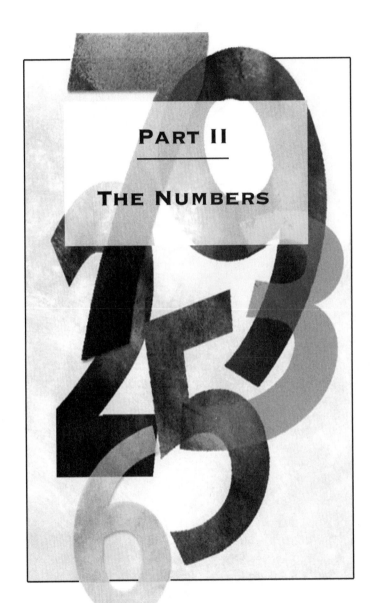

PART II

THE NUMBERS

An Analysis of the Numbers

This section is an exploration of what numbers mean, at a higher level than what we learned in Part I. We will look at analogies, and think about how to analyze each of the numbers, so we can learn their deeper meaning. Eventually we will learn to create charts that demonstrate how the numbers apply to our life.

0 - Zero

Analogies: Circle, sphere, neutrality, transparency, invisibility, absence of beginning and end, planet, atom, serpent, expansion, unknown, impracticable, nonexistent, infinity, non-created, intangible, origin, nothingness.

Analysis: Let us think about 0, not as a number, but as a numeric concept, since it expresses nonexistence and absence. Zero represents the abstract, the potential to be, something that is not —yet it contains the potential to be. It is also the glyph of stability in the abstract world, for its emptiness implies permanency. It is the very father of all numbers, since they only begin to exist in the moment they realize they do not exist. The consciousness of nonexistence can only refer to the past; if you do not exist, you cannot have such a consciousness. In the very moment you become conscious, you exist in the present, and being in the pre-existence period—the period number 0—is apprehended only as a fading memory.

Number 1 has the will of being the first that comes from 0's nothingness. Note that in the same way that number 0 generates number 1; 1 gives birth to all the other existing numbers.

There is no practical application for 0 in the chart, except for the challenges.[1] There is no "zero" person, so the number appears only as a transparent concept, such as 10, 20, 30, etc. But

---

1. You will learn about Challenges and other calculations that compound the numerological chart, in Part III.

it is funny to note how usual it is to write 01, 02, 03, and so on. That is one of the evidences of where elementary numbers come from. In the Tarot cards, 0 is the Fool, a character who is also associated with number 22 (2 – 2 = 0).

The *Tao Te Ching* expresses beautifully the universal function of zero through that quote:

> *The movement of the Tao consists in Returning.*
> *The use of the Tao consists in softness.*
>
> *All things under heaven are born of the corporeal;*
> *The corporeal is born of the Incorporeal.*[2]

1 - ONE

Analogies: Unity, men, virility, masculinity, activity, independence, aggressiveness, ego, Sun, victory, pioneering, leadership, authoritarianism, pride, selfishness, narcissism, tyranny, obstinacy, fire, gold, the father.

Analysis: This is the number representing the solar energy. It is very masculine, yang, and has all the related characteristics. The number 1 is not a number itself, but *the* number, since it portrays the totality connected to unity. It *is* everything, the unique, absolute, and the "great first." All the other numbers are an unfolding of 1, so he is the father of them all. Power is the point here; it is innate for 1, and whether that power is well used or not is another subject. It is most important to make clear that, no matter the lack or excess of power, dealing with it is the very aim of 1's existence, especially when it is about demonstrating that power. The "1 personalities" need some kind of reverence. Their vassals can get anything when they admit 1's authority, because the point is to play a game—and 1 always rules, for good or for

---

2. Lao Tzu, *Tao Te Ching*, John C. H. Wu, trans. (New York: St. John's University Press, 1961), Stanza 40, p. 59.

bad. Only then can 1 be generous and kind, as the sweetest king. But when that leadership is questioned, 1 will do anything to put the rebel in its "right" place. In that sense, 1 can be very naive: if one does not care about the official hierarchy, but only cares about results, one can easily convince the king of one's will, so the king will demand one's will as if it were his own. This kind of manipulation can be easily performed by certain personalities; it is the kind of persuasion that numbers like 2 have over some blind egos such as 1.

Each number has some positive and negative aspects, and composed numbers display particular tendencies, specifying a direction for the basic pattern represented by each elementary number. The principal origins for number 1 are 10, 19, and 28. The number 10, in its turn, is no more than an extension of 1's characteristics, since 0 works as an amplifier. Therefore, no modification happens in the essence of the number, for 0 is a transparent number, and it cannot modify anything except by amplification. Therefore, 10 represents a return to unity one level up on the spiral scale. Since 10 is even, the emphasized aspect of 1 is its softest side. The Pythagorean doctrine, according to Nicomano de Gerase,[3] regards 10 as a perfect number, the glyph of a deity, a symbol of the eternity as well as of the Sun,[4] see figure 4, page 30.

According to Lyses, the *tetractys* is the representation of pure harmony. Note that the triangular form means perfection and an equilibrium of polarities. The composition of 10 ($1 + 2 + 3 + 4 + 5 + 6 + 7 + 8 + 9 + 10$) is 55, emphasizing the sacred nature of the number, since it conceals a master number as its aim and direction.

The number 19 is extremely intense: it comes from 1, the beginning; and 9, the end; and results in 1 once again. It contains the alpha and the omega, which implies a great deal of strength

---

3. François-Xavier Chaboche, *Vida e Mistério dos Números* (São Paulo: Hemus, 1979), p. 157. As far as I know, this book is not available in English.
4. W. Wynn Westcott, *Numbers: Their Occult Power and Mystic Virtues* (London: Theosophical Publishing Society, 1902), pp. 90–92.

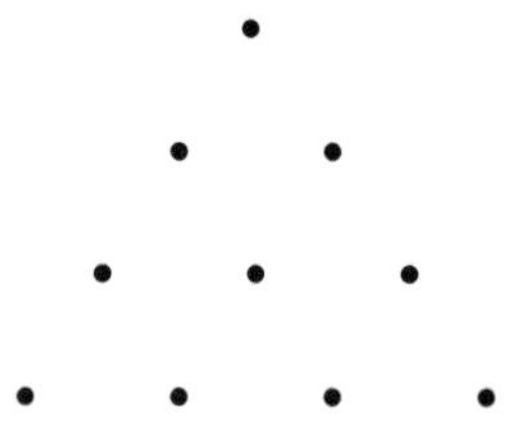

Figure 4. The tetractys.

and will—often used violently and blindly—which may give rise to a prodigy or a tragedy. Also, since the numbers are odd, it increases selfishness and vanity. So, 19 concentrates the dictatorial tendencies of 1, even though it may be channeled in a constructive way.

The number 28 is considered to be one of the best compositions for 1, since it is, mathematically speaking, a perfect number; that is, it is the result of its divisors. Perfect numbers are rare, only the first five are known: 6, 28, 496, 8,128 and 33,550,336.[5] That is enough to make 28 a concentration of 1's best possibilities. The number 28 is composed by two even numbers, which soothes 1's aggressiveness; while 8 is objective and practical—the balance of opposites in just one. The composition of the number points to 406, which adds up to 10 and then finally reduces to 1, so the circle is still going on. The determination of 1 in affirming personality is inherently manifested, whether or not it is channeled in a superior or in an inferior way. By the way, before astrologers realized that the zodiac was divided into 12 solar houses, there was another time division that was based on the Moon, and counted as 28.

The number 1 is linked to the fire element, since both represent power: prehistorical humans dominated wild animals right after they learned how to control fire. Through fire, human beings had the chance to rule the other animals, and even their

---

5. Jorg Sabellicus, *A Magia dos Números* (Lisboa: Edições 70, 1986), p. 25. This book is not available in English as far as I know.

own species. Even today, the owners of fire—that is, the owners of big arsenals—rule the world through war and/or technology. Fire is the manifestation of spirit and of intelligence over physical force. Humans were smaller, but they were still smarter than the dinosaurs; humans were afraid of fire, and that is why they had to dominate and control it. Alchemically, fire has a regenerating function. The myth of Prometheus displays 1's search for power. Prometheus dared to challenge the laws of Zeus and robbed fire from the Gods to give it to the human race. Prometheus was a prophet, and thus he knew that he was going to face the fury of Zeus. Zeus became angry about the theft, but at the same time he was scared, because being able to control fire would evolve humanity so they could become gods. As a punishment, Zeus condemned Prometheus to have his liver incessantly eaten by an eagle: as soon as the eagle finished eating the liver, it grew back again, inflicting endless pain on our hero. This torture continued until Zeus finally pitied Prometheus, and gave him back his freedom, at which point Prometheus, himself, became a God. This myth is a beautiful portrayal of the human hero journey on Earth. We can even trace parallels between it and Genesis. In this case, number 1 represents the whole of humanity.

2 - Two

Analogies: Duality, women, sensitiveness, femininity, passivity, dependency, tenderness, the Moon, receptiveness, diplomacy, humility, rhythm, collaboration, persuasion, cowardliness, submission, cruelty, negligence, shyness, lack of confidence, water, mother, silver.

Analysis: The number 2 represents duality, division, opposition, and is a complement to 1. Everything on our planet is dual: man and woman, clear and dark, hot and cold, good and evil. So, 2 symbolizes the very experience of existing as a human being on Earth. While 1 represents humankind, 2 is the sensation of being human, with all the conflicts and dichotomies that it carries within. The number 2 is the conscience of the contrasts of life. It is related to receptive people who work better when part of a duo instead of as a member of a group, or even all alone. These people always think about marriage, partnership, and things like this. The number 2 thinks "we," not "me." They prefer to have somebody around to tell them what to do; that's their way to be efficient. As the Moon reflects sunlight, 2 absorbs 1's energy and feeds itself from the excess of the generator of the light.

Some authors writing about numerology support a theory in which 2 is displayed as a diabolical number, for the sake of being the so-called destroyer of Sacred Unity, the killer of God. That is rubbish. It is naïve and superficial to associate negative-feminine-evil-demon like this. Everybody knows that light needs darkness just as darkness needs light, for we can only conceive one by comparing it with the other. Knowledge comes from comparing contraries, so we know that the same Sun that provides life can kill us by sunstroke; and the same water we drink when we are thirsty can kill us by drowning. So, forget Manicheanism. This way of thinking is a vice that comes from the superstitions propagated by the Medieval Church during the Dark Ages.

The greatest power in the number 2 lies in silence and intuition. In 2 begins the real counting, for when we have just one, there is nothing to count. It is also the beginning of rhythm, dance, statistics and music. Body is a division of the soul, which is originally androgynous, and as Hermes Trismegistos would say, "the kosmos and man are both dual, being visible or corporeal, and invisible and incorporeal. Man is also said to be dual in the sense that he is mortal and immortal. The seven cosmic or archetypal men were bisexual."[6] The division may connote separation, but this may be necessary for life experience, as well as for understanding duality. As it is said in Aleister Crowley's *Liber AL*, "For am I divided for love's sake, for the chance of union."[7]

---

6. Ruth Phelps, *The Universe of Numbers* (San Jose, CA: A.M.O.R.C., 1984), p. 65.

7. Aleister Crowley, *The Law is for All* (Phoenix: New Falcon, 1993), p. 47.

According to Philo, human beings are dual, consisting of a celestial (heavenly) part and a material (earthly) part.[8] That means that humans may be God or animal, or both at once. The concept of the Greek God Abrasax, who reunites in himself God and Demon, displays that nicely: unless there is harmony between those opposites, there's no *mysterium conjunctionis*, no son/daughter, no number 3.

Number 2 can be substituted in some cases by 11, for if we find an 11 in the middle of an operation, we must stop reducing the number. Therefore, the only composition you are going to find in your calculations will be 20, the number of regeneration that represents knowledge coming from past experiences that is to be projected into the future. It is also a number of conflicts caused by the awakening of conscience.

Water is the appropriate element for 2, since every liquid is passive and adaptable: a change of weather can change its state, turning it into solid (ice) or vapor. Also, water takes the form of whatever contains it. Life began and still begins in water; it is Isis's veil, the element of fecundity.

The composition of 2 is 3 (1 + 2 + 3), its aim and objective is procreating. Its biggest power is passivity, *à la* Gandhi. As the *Tao Te Ching* would say:

> *That which shrinks*
> *Must first expand.*
> *That which fails*
> *Must first be strong.*
> *That which is cast down*
> *Must first be raised.*
> *Before receiving*
> *There must be giving.*[9]

---

8. Ruth Phelps, *The Universe of Numbers*, p. 77.
9. Lao Tsu, *Tao Te Ching*, Gia-Fu Feng and Jane English, trans. (London: Wildwood House, 1973), stanza 36.

3 - Three

Analogies: Creativity, children, expansion, happiness, expression, art, diversification, sociability, communication, jealousy, pride, fakeness, evasion of energy, conversation, impracticability, air, inspiration, triangle.

Analysis: Since 1 represents the male and 2 represents the female, the connection between them represents the child, the son, the result of the union between opposite polarities. It is a number of synthesis and essence. It is the very representation of the Law of the Triangle, which is the law of equilibrium of differences through assimilation. The influence of this principle of 3 can be found in almost all religions and philosophies. You can check it out: you will find the universal mantra *AUM;* Father, Son and Holy Spirit for Christians; Sun, Moon and Earth for Earth religions; the three main letters of the Hebrew alphabet (aleph, mem, schin); Brahma, Vishnu, and Shiva for the Hindus; Osiris, Isis, and Horus for the Egyptians; Oddin, Frega, and Thor for the Scandinavians; Baal, Astarte, and Melkart for the Chaldeans; Ormuzd, Ahriman, and Mithra for the Persians. The Great Work is divided in three parts: the dark, the white and the purple work.[10]

There are three realms: mineral, vegetable, and animal. Time is divided in past, present, and future. It is also said in the writings of Hermes Trismegistus, "Therefore, I am called HERMES TRISMEGISTUS, having the three parts of the wisdom of the whole world. "[11]

People symbolized by number 3 have a dynamic temper and are always dealing with creativity, but they are not practical at all. It causes number 3 to lack organization, but that is supposed to be solved in the next step, number 4.

---

10. W. Wynn Westcott, *Numbers: Their Occult Power and Mystic Virtues.* See his work on number 3, pp. 40–46.
11. Ruth Phelps, *The Universe of Numbers,* p. 201.

The principal compositions of 3 are 12, 21, and 30. The three keep the basic characteristics of 3, such as creativity and communicability, but 12 is the slowest one, which does not mean 12 is not anxious. It carries a lot of anxiety internally, which may cause 12 to get frustrated—its inner time is faster than outer time. The composition 1 + 2 = 3 manifests the trinity through organization. It is a number of learning through cyclic experience. There is a section in the *Apocalypse* that mentions a tree of life, which produced fruits twelve times every month. Since the power of 1 is filtered through the slow motion of 2, there is not too much initial impact coming from 12. However, the effect of this number is noticeable, exactly because 12 turns everything into a pachydermatous slow vibration.

The number 21 projects 2's perception and subtlety through 1's roughness. This is the number of the world, because it accomplishes the male being occupied by the female, and the female being occupied by the male. It explains the fact that the 21st arcana of the tarot is portrayed with an androgynous center. And we can also think that 21 is the result of 3 x 7; that is, the trinity of wisdom, since 7 represents all (im)possible knowledge on Earth.

What more could I say about 30 other than that it works as 10 and 20, being a higher dissolution of the original number 3?

The associated element for 3 is air, because 3 is the inspiration needed for creation, and for imagination before creation, as well as the process of communication that facilitates materialization (that comes with number 4). Air is intangible, we cannot see it or touch it, but we feel its effect when we breathe, or when we feel the breeze touching our skin. Thoughts are also like this: we cannot see or hold them, but their effect is evident on people and on the world.

Blue is the color for communication. By the way, the chakra located between the larynx and the throat is supposed to be blue. This chakra is the ruler of voice and expression.

Once again, let's use the *Tao Te Ching* to illustrate the meaning of the number.

Tao begets one;
one begets two;
Two begets three;
three begets all things.[12]

4 - FOUR

Analogies: Solidity, organization, rationalization, restriction, work, rectitude, trustworthiness, honesty, patience, slowness, practicability, traditionalism, straightness, immutability, prejudice, repression, retardation, ignorance, limitation, sudden violence, square, earth, gray.

Analysis: From nowhere (0) comes the primordial unity (1), which was made (2), generating contrasts—these being harmonized by creation (3). But it was very necessary, anyway, that all the creative flux was turned into something practical, functional, and that wasn't happening because of a lack of organization (for 3 lets the ideas float in, barely putting them in order). For 3, organization would be death. For 4, it is pleasure. That is shown when we notice that there are 4 triangles inside a square, which is the symbol for 4. Just place an X inside the square and you'll see! That alludes to the qualities of organization and blocking. Systematic, persistent, 4 is even, yin, sensible, but yet very thorough and repetitive. It is like soft water that hits the hard rock for decades, finally making a hole in the rock through its enormous persistence. The number 4 represents the moment you must be firm about your aims. It is the foundation that everything lies on. That

---

12. Lao Tzu, *Tao Te Ching,* Ch'u Ta-Kao, trans. (London: Allen & Unwin, 1937), stanza 42. Footnote in this edition says, "Yen Fu says, 'Tao is the Primordial; it is absolute. In its descent it begets one. When one is begotten, Tao becomes relative, and two comes into existence. When two things are compared, there is their opposite, and three is begotten.'"

is why 4's element is earth, meaning "feet on the ground" and rationality. The so-called "number 4" people usually have stable tempers, but when they lose their calmness, we can expect an earthquake! Just like all the "yin" numbers, 4 is conservative and against. It also means that 4 prefers to walk by roads they already know, rather than finding new paths. Sometimes, it is difficult for 4 to get out of the tendency of classifying everything and not recognizing unique things and people—a tendency to be completely "normal," to the point of abnormality.

Generally, 4 indicates a trustworthy person. It is the salt of the earth, the craftsman. In the human body, 4 is related to the base of the body—the feet and legs. The very organization of the world takes place in a cycle of 4: there are 4 seasons (spring, summer, fall, winter); 4 cardinal points (east, west, north, south); 4 elements (fire, water, air, earth); 4 essential states (hot, wet, cold, dry); 4 basic mathematics operations (addition, subtraction, multiplication, division); 4 qabalistic worlds (the world of emanation, creation, formation, action); 4 temperaments (sanguineous, lymphatic, bilious, nervous) and so on.[13] Trismegistos wrote:

Its father is the Sun;
Its mother is the Moon;
The wind carries it in its womb;
And its nurse is the earth.[14]

The principal compositions for this number are 13 and 31. Everyone knows about the bad press that 13 carries. Poor number! It symbolizes death and/or a break, for sure, but that only sounds scary to our occidental ears, for we are used to understanding death as our end rather than as a transformation. The caterpillar's death is the birth of the butterfly. The human birth is the

---

13. W. Wynn Westcott, *Numbers: Their Occult Power and Mystic Virtues,* see his work on the esoteric meaning of the number 4, pp. 48–56.
14. Ruth Phelps, *The Universe of Numbers* (San Jose, CA: A.M.O.R.C., 1984), p. 201.

death of the soul, while the human death is the rebirth of the soul. That is why it is asked, in *Liber AL,* that we have a feast for birth, but a bigger one for death.[15] The number 13 is the projection of 1's will through the creative dynamics of 3, making a kind of unquiet 4 (which is almost a contradiction). Still, 4 is too different from this composition, so it may degenerate into laziness and pessimism, which are 4's worst aspects. Breaking up is part of growth, but if 13 becomes afraid, it will also get rotten. The message is kill to avoid being killed. The number 13 frequently indicates a fear of death, of losing, or even an obsession about these subjects. It can be a very benefic number, if one has quick reflexes and thoughts, and, most of all, if one is not lazy or too slow.

On the other hand, 31 represents something a little trickier, for it symbolizes a great obstacle, a big wall, a mountain to climb, the Dark Night of the Soul which comes before the Golden Dawn. The child (3) must cross alone (1) the obstacle (4). The child represents all of us in our moments of decision. This number can indicate big power and the courage face an archetypal obstruction. It also represents great frustration and blocking, when we fear and accept the blocking, for this is no more than an initiation. And if we compose 4, 13, or 31, we will always find 1. That's why 4 is a passive and yet thorough number.

5 - FIVE

Analogies: Freedom, independence, rebelliousness, adolescence, youth, changes, trips, progress, evolution, sexuality, the senses, pleasures, drugs, malice, drinks, fashion, futility, the pentagram, promiscuity, irony, fire, ether, red.

---

15. Aleister Crowley, *The Law is for All* (Phoenix: New Falcon, 1993), p. 54.

Analysis: After 4 had organized everything, it must have had some rebellion—that's life's economy, action, and reaction. The number 5 comes to break all the rules designed by 4; it is the adolescent who hates people telling him or her what and how to do, the iconoclast who loves to shock others and get a lot of attention. Since number 5 is 4's opposite, it can be nothing but unstable; it may be here now, but it may suddenly disappear. Its volatile characteristic makes it somewhat unfaithful, but also very charming, seductive and fun. The human senses are symbolized by 5, so it represents absorbing all these pleasures until satiety is reached. Therefore 5 symbolizes everything that may expand human consciousness. This is where its exacerbation of sex comes from—sex is the main form of conscious alteration. Also drugs are very important to 5, but an exaggeration of any kind can result in promiscuity, or a viciousness that is the shadow of the number, its most dense aspect.

The number 5 has no defined personality, let's put it like that. It represents people who hate labels and definitions, always trying to get out of them by changing all the time. Thus, 5 has the face of the moment, changing from happiness to sadness in a minute. A 5 person may say something right now, then deny it a week later, and finally forget the whole subject! It's like being a full-time actor, changing the personality and point of view while breathing. Number 5 tends to change into a new thing (or new ambient, new person), and after a time, it reacts and then changes into something else.

If you consider 5 as the conjunction of 2 (the first female number) and 3 (the first real male number, since 1 is an absolute number, capable of generation—it generates number 2 all alone, by fractioning itself), you will note a sexual implication. That is so because 5 is the result of 2 (the woman) and 3 (the first human male): an addition, the conjunction of the bodies with no necessary intention of procreation. Compare the addition 1 + 2, which portrays number 1, the semi-god, copulating with 2, the first human female, to have a baby, number 3, the first human male, the Elohim. It implies procreation, as well as the multiplication 2 x 3, producing 6, the glyph of the family. All this clarifies the fact that 5 is interested in the sexual act for what it is. Also, as a rebel, it does not accept rules and its will is to try everything *in loco*; it is a number that generally links to bisexuality, at least as an experience.

Some say there was a fifth planet in our solar system, which has exploded, leaving only some asteroids to replace it. Also 5 is related to the pentagram, the symbol of magick, protection, and its shape is that of the perfect human being. And note that the four fingers of the hand couldn't work well without the basis provided by the fifth, which is the only isolated and really different finger.

When we compose 5, it results in 15, reinforcing the tendency to passion, luxury, and lust; but with the guilt within—6, the resulting number. It is like a Catholic who does everything he is not supposed to, according to the regulations of his religion, but goes every Sunday to mass to "regret" his sins, thinking it is all right, and maybe it is, since each of us works in a particular system. There are two basic kinds of human being, according to Thelema: the stars—our natural condition, with their orbits and laws; and the planets—our degeneration, that surrounds a star, which can be presented as a person as well as an entity, a Deity, a thing, or any perceivable matter.[16]

Since it is a volatile number, trips and moving are related to it. Its principle compositions are 14, 23, and 32. Number 14 is an atypical 5, because of its chronic blocking, which may be drained through patience. Number 14 is the number of alchemy, the equilibrium between opposites. It does not come easily. The strong energy represented by 1 being expressed through 4's

---

16. Thelema is the name of the philosophy developed by Aleister Crowley and his students.

conservatism smashes its force, in a sense. Therefore, the 5 that comes from 14 has the typical anxiety of all 5s, but its rationalization gives a deeper mood to the number. You may think about 14 as the water in a dam that is going to break up sooner or later. The worst side of the number is the tendency to exaggerate in a radical way, like being the straightest person for a long time, and then all of a sudden losing control and going nutty, and then getting straight and square again, and so on. People associated with such a number should stimulate their need for change, but always try to be reasonable, otherwise they will float between self-denial and impulsiveness. This obsessive behavior may turn into a paradigm, and these people may think that human beings should use the senses, and not their finer sensibilities, such as intuition.

Number 23 suggests discretion, delicacy expressed through eloquence, which gives birth to an unquiet, yet consequential kind of number 5. Note that consequence is a rare quality in 5. Also 23 is a very vain emanation, but on the other hand, it is gifted with a great sense of humor. If you think about the natural development of 23, you will notice that the beginning of this emanation is more a 5 in the adolescent sense, and that as they develop they become more mature—always a 5, but more concerned about adult situations. Thus 23 is an "easy" number, in the sense that it follows the usual pattern of development (young-old).

Number 32, in its turn, is the reborn child, the baby (3) that falls in limbo (2) to reappear as an enhanced 5. This number represents the Golden Dawn attained found by those who surmount the obstacle of 31. There are 32 Qabalistic Paths of Wisdom. The shining of 3 is filtered by the gentleness of 2, but 32 may also symbolize great liars who are smooth talkers.

Number 5 is a fire number, a red one. It manifests great curiosity about anything hidden, esoteric, mysterious, exotic, and is linked to occultism and esotericism for that reason. It is a number of both fire and ether, the abstract element that originated all the others. This interest leads on to rituals, witchcraft, sexual magick, tantra, drug magick, paganism, and interests that are both positive and negative for the individual.

6 - SIX

Analogies: Harmony, sociability, the search for perfection and conciliation, family, stability, solicitude, responsibility, care, fidelity, jealousy, possessiveness, loathing, intermission, conservatism, indecision, dependency, bad judgment, water, green.

Analysis: As every following number reacts against its antecessor, the social iconoclasm of 5 has its counterpoint in 6's traditionalism. While 5 needs to contest, 6 needs to accept. It is a "family" number, and its affections have deep roots. Number 6 represents people looking for perfection, but not in the sense that number 7 would take it. Let us say that 7 actually *finds* a certain kind of perfection; while 6 *looks for it,* being too partial in its concerns to get even close to perfection. Number 6 is seeking social acceptance, and its conception of perfection is linked to the concept that the voice of the people is the voice of God. That is, if you are socially accepted, you are well; if not, you are a pariah, which is the worst thing to be for a 6. Note that both 5 and 6 mean adaptation to actual circumstances, but in different ways: 5 clones itself into what's going on in a radical way; while 6 tries to use common sense, diplomacy, and taking the middle path, which may involve wisdom as well as hypocrisy. Number 6 doesn't want any kind of polemic, maybe because it is a mathematically perfect number, the result of the addition of its divisors (1, 2, 3). Besides, 6 can also be the result of those numbers multiplication, confirming its popularity. Number 6 needs to be on good terms with everyone, which is not possible.

Number 6 is also the result of 2 (female) multiplied by 3 (male), making the family: the man and woman multiply, and they generate babies. Notice that sex has a procreative function for 6; while for 5, sex is basically for pleasure.

All the trinitarian numbers, such as 3, 6, and 9 are linked to communication, art and expression. Number 6 is not as creative as 3, but it is more productive. The Pythagoreans said that 6 is the perfection of the parts, and, after a period of 216 years (the cube of 6), all things are regenerated.[17]

People represented by this number are usually very humanitarian. According to Genesis, God created man at the 6th day. The 6th sense reunites the 5 "real" senses, plus an abstract-extra one.

The searching for stability in love can turn into possessiveness, when the person trying to preserve the object of his or her affection ends up caging it. On the other hand, this is the most faithful number, which explains its reaction against anything new.

Its principal compositions are 15, 24, and 33. Number 15 represents the most instinctive, passionate, and daring kind of 6. As a result of 3 x 5, it is a very hybrid number 6, mixing lasciviousness with guilt, providing high doses of sensuality and aggressiveness. On the other hand, 24 is very different, for it is a fully feminine number, composed of 2 and 4, which are both weak in some cases. That is not exactly a good influence on 6, which is already way too sentimental. Thus, 24 is a very particular number, in its weakness and vulnerability. It emphasizes the worst aspects of 6, such as jealousy and a lack of confidence. Still, this is not necessarily a curse, or a pessimistic point of view. If you take it for what it is, 6 reflects nothing but a person being driven by some imaginary drama 24 hours a day, and there are several ways of dealing with that, all of them forms of channeling such a drama. The number 24 is the double of 12, and 12 is a number of sacrifice, and 24 is a kind of martyrdom. Number 24 errs because of its insistence, knowing previously about the error. That's the main difference between 12 and 24: 12 is learning, while 24 is martyring itself. And 33 symbolizes the liberation of it: a very

---

17. W. Wynn Westcott, *Numbers: Their Occult Power and Mystic Virtues*, p. 64.

refreshing spiritual enlightenment, yet also so intense that it can even be frightening, as looking directly into the Sun with the naked eye can be a blinding experience.

If you compose those numbers, all of them end in 3, reaffirming everything.

7 - SEVEN

Analogies: Intelligence, prudence, sobriety, study, meditation, erudition, analysis, philosophy, deepness, spirituality, religion, criticism, introspection, isolation, cynicism, malice, coldness, ancient, old, tradition, air, brain.

Analysis: 7 is the only number among the first ten that is neither a multiple nor a divisor of any other number. Number 1 would be an exception to this rule, nevertheless 1 is not *a* number, but *the* number, as we discussed earlier. This shows something about 7's personality: it has an enormous tendency to become isolated, apart from all that is going on around, as if the 7 was always outside the situation, analyzing and criticizing.

Spirituality is usually associated with calmness for some reason. The fact is that 7 is probably the most important number for every religious system. It is the number of the vital cycles of Earth: 7 days of the week, 7 days for each Moon; the renovation of human cells that happens in cycles of 7; there are 7 notes; 7 colors in the rainbow; 7 chakras; 7 orifices in the human face representing the 7 senses and the struggle for wisdom. According to Genesis,[18] creation took 7 days, and the seventh was not specifically a creation day, but a day of resting and of meditation on what had been created. Some Pythagoreans wrote that 7, being composed of 3 and 4, means the union of human and divine. And the Christians say that, when somebody asked Jesus if we were

---

18. We are using *The New English Bible with Apocrypha* (New York: Oxford University Press, 1971).

supposed to forgive 7 times, he answered, "I do not say seven times; I say seventy times seven."[19] By the way, the Apocalypse refers to 7 churches, 7 candelabra, 7 stars, 7 trumpets, 7 horns, 7 cups, 7 angels, 7 seals, 7 flagellants, a dragon with 7 heads, and a lamb with 7 eyes.

Its principal compositions are 16 and 25, obviously representing opposites. Number 16 is like a cutting thunder sweeping away all the dirt and destroying everything that is anti-natural, even when we are used to it; very like Shiva, the personality in charge of the ignorance and destruction in the material world, according to the Bhagavad-Gitā.[20] Number 16 destroys only what is already rotten; it is almost always a destruction "for good," regardless how unpleasant it may be when it happens. To resist the destruction is the worst thing to do when dealing with a 16, for it makes one accumulate waste. The suffering comes from attachment. But there are some aspects of 16 that would be the worst of 7, such as fanaticism, skepticism, depression, and pessimism. On the other hand, 25 reflects another side of 7, its most intuitive and daring aspect, mixing dualism and mutability. People related to 25 appear to have lots of self-control, but they have a melting volcano inside, going from one extreme to another, similar to the 5.

If you compose 7 $(1 + 2 + 3 + 4 + 5 + 6 + 7)$, you will find 28, the perfect number; 16 results in 136/10; and 25 = 325/10, all them 1, reinforcing 7's individuality. I used to call 7 "the false yin," because, even being masculine-yang-odd and everything, it still apparently shows weakness and fragility. That is so because of its introspection and low profile, which are easily misunderstood as shyness. But make no mistake, 7 is a thorough number, a discreet one, but very resistant and mentally strong.

---

19. "The Gospel According to Matthew," 18:22.

20. For those unfamiliar with the Gita, there are many versions available. One has been translated by Antonio de Nicolás, *The Bhagavad Gita* (York Beach, ME: Nicolas–Hays, 1990).

Number 7's basic expression is, "Why?" It has a strongly philosophic nature. That is both the root of its knowledge and the basis of its intellectualism. Anything ancient and ancestral attracts 7, a number that symbolizes tradition, old times, and lost civilizations.

8 - EIGHT

Analogies: Justice, adjustment, material affairs, karma, truth, correction, logic, objective, prosperity, realization, administration, linearity, militarism, power, ambition, vengeance, oppression, violence, earth, bones, law, right.

Analysis: While 7 represents mind and spirit, 8 represents body and matter, money, wealth, health. If we compare their temperaments, 7 would be the employee, and 8 the boss. After 7 conquers the domain of the mind, 8 comes to assure the maintenance of matter, taking care of the bills, and caring for the body to keep it healthy. Matter is not the enemy of spirit. That is like saying that night is the enemy of the day, and clearly reflects a fear of something that is not yet controlled. Some people try to control what they fear. It is futile to say "matter does not exist" when the thing itself is by your side, available to be touched and recognized. Still, you can have many points of view on the actual thing. Matter has been vilified by many Christian religious groups who forget that when dealing with the many aspects of matter it is part of our spiritual and material growth. The number itself shows this so clearly, for 8 is the number of matter and ambition, but it also is a mobius strip, ∞, infinity, connecting infinity with the finite. Matter is one path to spirit.

Of course some aspects of 8 are not that noble, for it can also be extremely greedy as well as repressive and demanding. Sometimes a degenerated 8 forgets about the earlier path, the 7th path, the one of mind and soul. When this happens, 8 gets as artificial and empty as a bored rich person. There's an old Greek proverb that says, "all the things are 8."[21] It is a false yin, the very opposite for the 7, the false yang. Number 8 looks like a shark, and can be as aggressive (and stupid) as a shark. Still, 8's attacks are actually a way of self-defense. Sometimes, a lack of confidence may produce a winner: some people desperately need to achieve because they can hide themselves behind their realizations. Number 8 wears an armature and looks enormous, but it is in reality hiding inside. The effort of carrying the armature as a second skin is what causes 8's typical tension. Some "8" people may be addicted to occasional big explosions as a way of channeling all that unreleased tense energy.

The principal compositions for 8s are 17 and 26. The first one is considered auspicious, for it is related to the Egyptian Goddess Nuit, the goddess of the night, whose body is the home of the stars. In 17, the main impulse characterized by 1 lies in a propitious yang polarity—as it happens with the numbers comprehended between 10 and 19. This vigorous energy is channeled through 7, which is yang—but a false yin—that solves any misplacing problem, and also gives 1 more concentration. The resulting 8 is more centralized than the one composed of 2 and 6, which incurs the same problem of 24: 26 is fully yin, 2 being the ruler of the concept that goes through 6 and ends at 8. If you visualize the numbers as an interconnection, you will perceive the weakness of this combination. Nevertheless, one can find force and illumination in walking those paths of 24 and 26, but that would be the case of a very specific nature, capable of ruling a dark hole, which is what those numbers are. They have no matter in their composition; they have anti-matter, a reaction to matter, not the non-existence of matter itself, which would be a designation more appropriate to number 0.

---

21. W. Wynn Westcott, *Numbers: Their Occult Power and Mystic Virtues,* p. 82.

9 - NINE

Analogies: Triple trinity, evolution, impulse, development, dynamism, creativity, liberalism, philanthropy, internationality, limitlessness, sympathy, rushing, acting, exaggeration, snooping, nervousness, dissipation, emotionalism, fire, vision, megalomania.

Analysis: This number displays the end of the archetypal journey of the essential numbers. After 9, all the numbers are repetitions of the essential archetypes, except the master numbers 11 and 22, which are *transformations* of those essential ones. This quality of transformation and development is intrinsically related to 9, for if we add 9 to any other number, the result will be a composed number that, when decomposed, will be the same first number again. Like 7 + 9 = 16, and 1 + 6 = 7. So, when 9 works with another number, it pushes the number toward the next step. It is a very evolutionary number, but it may also be invasive, for the sake of helping people who don't want any help at all.

Even with all the humanitarian qualities associated with 9, we should not forget that it is a yang number; that is, it involves a big ego. That gets more evident when you think that, if you multiply any number by 9, the result will always come back to 9. Like 9 x 5 = 45 = 4 + 5 = 9. If we also add the extremities of all the other essential numbers, we will have 9 again, as you can see in figure 5.

The number 9 represents divine manifestation on three levels: the world of the soul, the world of the mind, and the world of matter. It is also an essential number for Druid cosmogony, as one

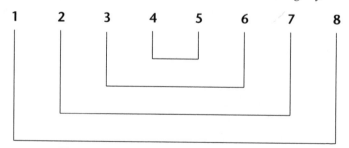

Figure 5. The extremities of essential numbers.

may notice by the 81 Triads, which are the basis of the study of that system. Since 9 is the result of 3 x 3, it manifests the Triple Trinity, being an energetic and magnetic number. People reflected by 9 tend to be restless and impetuous, never boring, but easily bored. This number contains in itself all the previous archetypes, so these people can't really be prejudiced. For them, the soldier and the president are quite the same, because in a sense 9 contains the qualities of both and more. This quality accelerates a tendency toward exaggeration and megalomania, but it is easy to forgive when you understand that 9 is the number that pushes the other numbers to "grow up." It is not a discreet number at all; it loves a scene, behaving as if the streets are a virtual stage.

Since 9 represents a borderline, it also represents crossing it; aren't borderlines made to be crossed? There are no limits for 9, not enough languages to learn, not enough countries to travel, not enough people to meet, never enough. When a 5 meets a 9, wait for moving, changing, sudden decisions and things of that nature.

The principal compositions are 18 and 27. The first one is regarded as sinister, but if you love the night you will not agree. Number 18 represents the darkness of the unconscious, the Pandora's box inside us all, containing fear, insecurity, hate, lust, envy, greed—all the feelings we tend to deny and hide. Denying them fortifies these feelings, and because we cannot deal with something we may pretend it doesn't exist. With 18, we can face all these things, for it is a good chance to overwhelm any problem related to our darkest side. Both demon and angel are parts of us, and the fear of darkness is the fear of our own inner demon. As it is said in a book called *O Caibalion:* "For the pure one, everything is pure; as for the vile, everything is vile and corrupted."[22] It is very common to find the number 18 in charts of

---

22. Rosabis Camaisar, trans. *O Caibalion* (São Paulo: Pensamento, 1978). I don't think this book is available in English. There are many books written about the kabbalah (spelled cabala, quabalah, kabalion, etc.) and students of number would do well to study the subject to better understand the symbology I mention here. Several authors published by Weiser are Halevi, Kaplan, Crowley, Fortune, Levi, and Gray, all coming from a different perspective.

religious leaders, which means that their darkest side projected them to the search of the light. Number 18 is also related to 666 (6 + 6 + 6 = 18), a number that alternates both sacred and profane aspects, depending on one's point of view. On the other hand, 27 is the one who calms 9 down (if that is possible), because the slowness of 2 mixed with 7's reasonability produces a grounded number 9, which expands itself without anxiety.

11 - Eleven

Analogies: Revelation, originality, timelessness, exoticism, inspiration, idealism, extravagancy, modernism, fanaticism, craziness, folly, illumination, incomprehension, difficult communication, degradation, air, a new millennium.

Analysis: This is one of the most complex and fascinating numbers. Polemic, regarded as cursed by some and sacred by others, its nature is volatile and indefinable. Two number 1s compose 11; it has a double male component, but if it were to be reduced, it would be the glyph of femaleness, 2. It brings a very mixed, ambiguous, even androgynous symbolism. It is easy to recognize an 11 energy going on, because even though the 11 male may be androgynous in some sense, he is never really feminine. The same happens about 11 women, because 11 cannot live in any ghetto, and doesn't feel comfortable being labeled, for mystery is part of its fascination.

Number 11 is always the one in the front of the front, very avant-garde, always anticipating in the present the tendencies of the future. It is the number of revelation: there were 11 faithful apostles who propagated Christ's message.[23] Still, the so-called anti-Christian *Book of the Law* quotes Nuit: "My number is 11, as all their numbers who are of us."[24] However, the bad press for 11 in esoteric and religious circles is as hysterical as the one about

---

23. Jorg Sabellicus, *A Magia dos Números*, p. 36.
24. Aleister Crowley, *The Law is for All*, p. 50.

number 2: this is a prejudice developed from the same sources. It is not a coincidence that the numbers representing the Great Mother are demonized by our present-day male-oriented society and religious systems. The Jews, for example, know that 11 is the number of Lilith—and some hate it because of that, since Lilith is associated with female insubordination toward the male. She was the first wife of Adam, created before (or with) him. According to Barbara Black Koltuv, Lilith is like a renegade instinct sent by God to live in the lower regions—that is, with humans.[25] The way we regard humanity will define what we are and what we will be, thus if we regard ourselves as the lowest creatures living in the lower side, what are we going to be?

Number 11 means illumination and/or insanity. Traditional qabalists link it to the 11 Adverse Sephiroth. Dion Fortune wrote, "The formulas used by Crowley would be considered as adverse and malefic by traditional qabalists, because he uses 11 instead of 10 as the number of groups of beatings in magic ceremonies, and 11 is the number of the Qliphoth or Demonic Sephiroth; therefore, a group of 11 beatings is an invocation of the Qliphoth."[26] Catholics think it is the number of sin and penitence, for it exceeds the number of commandments (10), while it is less than 12, which for Christians is a number of grace and perfection. Saint Augustine allegedly said that 11 is the insignia of sin.[27] However, it is the result of 5 and 6, union of microcosm and macrocosm, represented by the hex-pentagram, the symbol used by Masons. Pythagoreans have written that 11 marks the beginning of a higher level of consciousness. So we conclude that this number, just like any other force, can be well or badly applied. This is the path of the goat or the serpent.

---

25. Barbara Black Koltuv, *The Book of Lilith* (York Beach, ME: Nicolas-Hays, 1986), see pp. 20–26.
26. Dion Fortune, *Applied Magic* (London: The Aquarian Press, 1981), p. 65; reissued by Samuel Weiser, 2000.
27. François-Xavier Chaboche, *Vida e Mistério dos Números*, p. 161.

People represented by 11 are usually intrepid, original, arrogant, and different. They don't care about being friendly or not; they just are who they are, whoever they may be! They are channels of intuition and telluric energy.

Its main composition is 29, a softest 11, more gentle and sociable, but not enough to be considered "normal." Number 11 runs toward 66, the number of equilibrium and perfection, while 29 goes to 407, to return to 11 once again.

This is the true number of the new age, the new era. Eliphas Levi wrote, "11 is the number of force; it is that of strife and martyrdom. . . . Christ died between two thieves, and He took one of them with Him to Heaven."[28]

22 - Twenty-Two

Analogies: Lack of concern, detachment, passivity, cooperation, realization, philanthropy, dissolution, audacity, intensity, work, obstacles, repression, incapacity, ruin, megalomania, wisdom, intuition, perception, logic, idealism, water, accomplishment.

Analysis: This is the second and last number that we are not supposed to reduce or decompose. Its shadow is 4, and since 22 is a very high and difficult vibration to achieve, it may be "easier" to "be" a number 4, instead of developing 22's peculiar talents. The mission of 22 is very specific, for the obstacles are so many that only a spiritual mountaineer like 22 could take that path. And if 22 is not, if it decides to use its number 4 qualities instead of its real 22 talents, it is like a specialist pretending not to understand his or her own field of knowledge. One has the freedom to do so, and I defend this right; but, no matter what, it is a waste when people marked by number 22 get scared of being extra-brilliant, too cosmopolitan, profound and interesting—in a universal

---

28. Eliphas Lévi, *The Key of the Mysteries* (London: Rider, 1959; New York: Samuel Weiser, 1971), p. 42.

way—which is its main difference with 4, who may be all these things, too, but in a silent and local way. When it happens the opposite way, megalomania rules. In this event, the vision turns into delirium, and prudence, typical to 4, should be recommended.

You can tell that 22 is a radical number. Number 11 is radical, too, but this first master number controls everything around, subtly, while 22 is controlled by it; it is a tunnel for the wind to pass through, as any female number must be. Both are kind of "a man with a mission," but 11 wants to take control of it, while 22 doesn't need to ask anything. For 22 it is enough just to close the eyes and let a power speak through.

Number 22 symbolizes the act of taking care of others in a transcendental way. Its power is basically an anti-power, a veiled power, not an explicit one—passivity as a way to be active. It is devotion as an instrument of liberation. We can say that this number represents the denying of the lower self as a way to affirm the higher self. That would—and could—be a way of illumination. But let's just meditate on the perfection of imperfect things: 22 suffers, theoretically, from the same problem of 24 and 26, which is being fully even and passive. The only difference is that there is not a 22 result (if there were, it would be 4), so the yin influence doesn't work in the same way as those problematic numbers. Since 22 is a master number, it deals with this passivity problem on different levels. One of these ways is to be passive, just to emphasize the defect as much as possible, and that may produce an illumination. This is the path of the lamb, or the pigeon. The conjugation of the paths of pigeon and serpent will form the Path of Abrasax, 33.

There are 22 major arcana in the tarot; 22 number-letters in the Hebrew alphabet; 22 chapters in the Apocalypse. According to Isidoro de Seville, God created 22 things in the six days of creation: on the first day, the shapeless matter, the angels, the light, the higher skies, earth, water and air; on the second day, the firmament; on the third day, the seas, seeds, herbs, trees; on the fourth day, the Sun, Moon, and the planets; on the fifth day, the fishes, the aquatic reptiles, the terrestrial reptiles and the birds; and on the sixth day, the beasts, domestic animals, and men.[29]

People with 22 in their charts are normally very progressive and successful, but they can also be extremely blocked and tense. Sometimes 22 people speak as if they owned the whole world's truth, but they are actually very generous and just want to share it with everyone. Still, their megalomania can build them up and/or make dust of them.

In the Bhagavad-Gītā, chapter 8, verse 22, it is said that the Supreme Personality of God, who is bigger than anything, is only reachable through pure devotion.

Additional Numbers

Let's see, succinctly, some other composed numbers. This is not a deep vision about these numbers, but it will be enough to initiate you into basic symbolism that should be considered when working with these numbers.

34/7: The search for independence; leadership, creativity, elitism, crudeness, criticism, intelligence, method, rigor, formality, impatience. People symbolized by 34 are fast when beginning something, but do not maintain the rhythm, getting slow and weak easily.

35/8: Expansion, growing up, development, great ambition, vanity, wealth, fluency, an attractive person, ambiguity, yang/yin equilibrium, changes, dynamism, modernity, arrogance, narcissism.

36/9: Fulfillment, totality, universality, determination, insistence, imagination, adaptability toward obstacles, compassion, inconsequence. The sacred number used by Pythagoreans to

---

29. Jorg Sabellicus, *A Magia dos Números*, p 37.

swear fidelity. The composition of 36 results in 666, the number of the magic square[30] of the Sun.

37/10/1: Independence, fearlessness, boldness, leadership, mentally powerful, maturity, implacability, fertile imagination, self-centered, egocentric, even rough, theoretical, dominance.

38/11: Intuition, vision, capacity of adapting revolutionary ideas to the mainstream, wealth, mixture of creative and business talent, prophetic dreams, risk of self-indulgence, deep perception of subtle energies.

39/12/3: Romanticism, delicacy, a sense of humor, maturity, disposition, theoretical better than practical, delay, community, research, knowledge. This is a number of tranquility and placidity, coming from 12, but still in an intense way, provided by 39.

40/4: This number announces the advent of blocks and obstacles, yet they come for good; they will help to develop knowledge and bring a sense of opportunity. Purification before realization: Jesus is supposed to have been in the desert for 40 days before his enlightenment. Organization, discipline, works for getting power and domain, traditionalism, inflexibility, breaks.

41/5: Versatility, adaptability, courage, sons and daughters; a solid basis, security even when taking risks; daring, potency, fertility, dreams to make true. Success may deteriorate the personality.

42/6: Qabalists say that this is the number of letters contained in God's true name. Strong base maintaining fragility, like an iron pedestal for a crystal glass. Possessiveness, jealousy and all the problems of a fully even composed number, as you must know at this point. But the number 4 in the yang position is less bad than 2 in the same position as it is in 24.

---

30. P.-V. Piobb, *Formulário de Alta Magia* (Rio de Janeiro: Francisco Alves, 1982), pp. 165–174.

43/7: Roots, solidity, powerful mind, authority, intelligence, diplomacy, vacillation, hesitation; beginning is always difficult for 43; it takes time to articulate the first movements; constancy, parsimony; a trustworthy person; discretion; strong health—despite a tendency toward vice.

44/8: The power of the earth, the base, resistance, persistence, patience, credibility, exigency. Number 44 must fight a lot before it gets what it wants. Prudence, materialism, skepticism, prejudice, illusion. May have problems with gluttony.

45/9: Mysticism, anxiety, dynamism, restlessness, distant communication, psychic energy, influential friends, sons and daughters, precipitation.

46/10/1: Material power, strength, social influence, dealing with law and papers, demanding but not a dictator, nepotism, preoccupation, smartness, persuasion, spontaneity.

47/11: Intuition, but with a tendency to rationalize and consequently, destroying it; lack of spontaneity. May be an interesting emanation, if one is aware of its dichotomy and tries to concentrate in 11's aims, better than the seriousness of 4 and 7 conjoined, which can be really suffocating to an 11's mind.

48/12/3: Slowness, anxiety, laziness, waste of opportunities, lack of self-esteem. A kind, gentle yet shy and hesitating person.

49/13/4: Adverse conditions turn into success—the result of a great obsession; 49 is always helped by somebody or something, in a strange and spontaneous way. May get in trouble because of its vicious tendencies. Sensitivity masked by rudeness; as well as great ambition hiding behind the face of humility.

50/5: Libido, sexuality, sensuality, impassivity, lasciviousness, trips, moving, internationalism, inconstancy. Tendency to get things easily and to lose them easily as well. Alternate periods of reclusiveness and sociability.

51/6: Creativity, art, eloquence, a fighter, a troublemaker, an argument, battle, law, sacrifice (but with a reward), too arrogant; brilliant yet impatient mind; uncertainty due to too much pretension.

52/7: Authoritarianism, anxiety, rushes. Meditates easily, and 52 needs meditation to help solve inner conflicts; may be rude, stingy, or cold.

53/8: People who want to make lots of things at the same time, and eventually manage multiple things at once; 53 looks disorganized, but there is a method under the apparent disorder. Rationality, objectivity, preciosity, a detailer, challenge, courage, expansion.

54/9: There are some blocks that must be pushed away so fluency and spontaneity can flow naturally for 5 and 9. Confusion as the result of lack of control and guilt; needs to recognize its own impulses first, and then to provide an outlet for them.

55/10/1: Great energy, agitation, trips, communicability, persuasion, sexuality, pioneering, exuberance, smartness, wiliness, irony, cynicism. Interest in religion and metaphysics.

56/11: Powerful number, microcosm plus macrocosm, perfect intuition, balance, originality, right decision, esthetic sense. Should avoid delay and indecision, for such things would empty the intrepid energy of this number.

57/12/3: Hidden impulsiveness. Dichotomy between intention and action. It is apparently parsimonious, but actually passionate. Wise and intelligent, 57 represents the one who easily understands another's point of view. Charity, sacrifice, fears.

58/13/4: Introspection, egocentrism, pause, stop, solitude, readjustment causing transformation. Must work in order to canalize its intense energy of realization. Tends to obsessive habits that may damage health. Conclusion, understanding, perception.

59/14/5: Ups and downs, instinctive energy, sex, games, risks, adventure. An agile mind. Irresponsibility, lack of compromise, cowardice.

60/6: Social balance, harmony, tranquility, esthetic, health, wedding, relationship, results, fertility, imagination, playfulness, sweetness, compassion.

61/7: The fear of being discovered. Repression, hidden emotions, isolation, fears linked to religion or witchcraft, has the intelligence to deal with insecurity. Beware of undercover people. The number is linked to AIN, the negative existence of the Deity.[31]

62/8: Impasse, stagnation, restriction, delay, passivity. This is a mature number, which insists on behaving emotionally, pretending to be naïve. Should avoid building castles in the sand.

63/9: Balance, reformation, mission, missionary, creation, art, independence, regenerating quality. A person who may be too idealistic.

64/10/1: Great character, strong personality, consequence, materialization, hard work, organization, method, hierarchy, determination, magnetism, truth. May be ruined by the tricks of the ego, tough.

65/11: Solid basis allows one to take risks with the guarantee of protection. This is the number of Adonai, the Holy Guardian Angel. Charisma, silence, elevation, growing, building.

66/12/3: Security, stability, communication, expression, family, responsibility. Moralist, but exceedingly sweet, affable and popular people come under the symbolism of this number.

---

31. W. Wynn Westcott, *Numbers: Their Occult Power and Mystic Virtues*, p. 93.

67/13/4: Symbolizes the alternation of periods, when in a moment lots of things happen suddenly and at once, and periods when nothing happens at all. May represent a threat. Work, rigidity, fear, difficulty in dealing with money. If it learns how to avoid being pretentious, can be very productive.

68/14/5: Materialism, seeks security excessively. Avoids risks, loses lots of things with that, avoiding along with the risks also any possibility of growing up, so this may be the symbol for blocking development.

69/15/6: Emotional, impulsive, lascivious, loving, partial, intense. Anticipation. Every day is like the last day. Luxury, ostentation, comfort. This number works exclusively under the edge of lust, even when it is not about sex.

70/7: Seriousness, rigor, introspection, critical analysis. Tends to power abuse, which happens when 7 loses its self-criticism. Should keep secrets, for this is its greater quality.

71/8: Honor, nobility, construction, opportunities, taciturnity, reticence, serious, interested. Stable through ups and downs.

72/9: Theory diverges from practice; difficulty being objective; contradiction between speech and attitude. Confusion, sensitivity, capacity for transmutation, mercy.

73/10/1: Wisdom, centralization, fatherhood, control, egocentrism, generosity, conscience, lucidity, teacher, prudence. A philosophical mind at the service of ambition.

74/11: Tends to destroy the intuitive process. Strong perception should be channeled in the right way, because the great power of this mind would badly affect the environment if it concentrates on evil thoughts.

75/12/3: Searches for freedom of speech but tends to self-censorship. Should work hard to have the desired result, which is not a modest one. Creative talent and latent communicability.

76/13/4: May be easily manipulated by others. Excessive humility covering cowardice or insecurity. Great capacity for organization and regeneration. A 76 person knows the way to go, but hesitates, feeling his or her feet attached by roots.

77/14/5: Psychological and/or magick knowledge, which may be misused. Great charisma can guide this person through unsuspected heights.

78/15/6: Cause and effect, calculated risks, intelligence, communication, firmness, extroversion and sense of opportunity—or even opportunism.

79/16/7: Anxiety and precipitation that may destroy what was made to succeed. Tends to be pushy and force things. Humility not to be confused with humiliation.

80/8: Noble character, progress, wealth, conquering, expansion, justice, adjustment, favorable decisions, integrity, dignity, impartiality, exaggerated rigor.

81/9: Impulsive, growing, evolution, dispute of egos, conflict that can be very productive and yield good results. Anxiety under control.

82/10/1: Defined aim, step-by-step ascension, conscience of own qualities and defects, success, determination, discreet leadership.

83/11: Connection, information, freshness, capacity for influencing people, bold ideas adapted to ordinary thought, undercover infiltration in hostile environment. The comprehension of the Absolute.

84/12/3: Fear, apprehension, preoccupation, confounds rationalism with pessimism. Behaves like "the victim." Wants attention. It is better than it appears to be; its worrying blinds its kindness as well as other qualities.

85/13/4: Flexibility, adaptability, mutability, laziness, pessimism, exoticism, extravagance, sudden changes, work, effort, hidden authoritarianism, imagination.

86/14/5: Hypocrisy, lies, impulsiveness, can fake something naturally and easily, innocuous activities. Hides a volcano inside.

87/15/6: Instincts are in reason's service; intellect, capacity to evolve, dynamism, speed, luxury, comfort, wealth, ostentation, and inheritance.

88/16/7: Pragmatism, dogmatism, fanaticism. A big head. Repressive, tension, rigidity, pessimism.

89/17/8: Wealth, materialism, generosity, hope, logic, quick thought, agility, prize, benefice, intolerance, impatience.

90/9: A person who deeply understands ambiguity in people and things. Regeneration.

91/10/1: Alternation between benevolence and dictatorship. Dualism and flexibility. A dominating personality tormented by guilt, which makes him or her suffer bouts of depression and enthusiasm. Both periods should be used in the proper way, extracting the best of each polarity.

92/11: Plenitude, achievement, spiritual force, intuition. An ahead-of-the-times personality. Weirdness enhanced with sweetness, gentleness, and diplomacy. Good dealing with conservatives, even though 11 is always a rebel.

93/12/3: Privations and sacrifices are rewarded, development, help through friends, maturity, happiness in difficult moments. Faces any challenge with serenity and sense of humor.

94/13/4: Evolutionary impulse blocked by reticence. Abortion. Regeneration. Pessimism and insecurity faking arrogance.

95/14/5: Scary but inoffensive instincts, which can make one afraid of his or her own shadow. May go far to avoid the tendency to get paralyzed when afraid.

96/15/6: Passion, romance, lasciviousness, wedding or union related to work or matter. Lack of control caused by emotionalism.

97/16/7: All or nothing. Devastating failure or great success, great intelligence or enormous lack of capacity.

98/17/8: Material and professional success, tranquillity, hope, sometimes confused but always reasonable.

99/18/9: The capacity for generation, in an amplified way. Evolution, confusion, and anxiety turns all matters into something bigger than they actually are.

100/1: Formidable change, evolution, strong character. Person apparently has a sweet temper, but hides a very dominant personality. Noble.

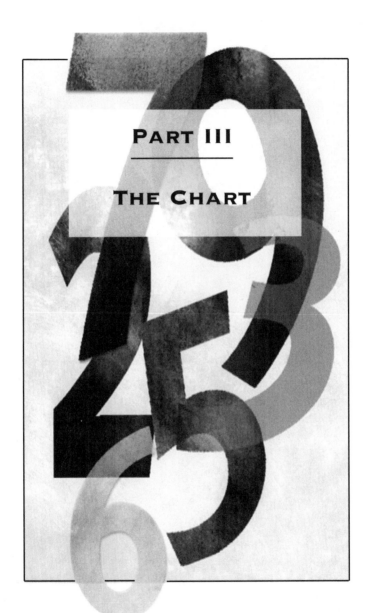

PART III

THE CHART

JOHN LENNON'S CHART

Now, let's learn, step-by-step, how to calculate and interpret a numerological chart, according to the system given in the last section. The system is logical, but very subtle, so you will have to really digest the meaning of the number combinations.

In numerology, the name represents the personality, it means "who." The birth date means "how." It is the road where the name is walking, the so-called "destiny." That is to say, the personality includes your feelings, behavior, characteristics, the way you react when facing various situations, your choices and will; while destiny includes key situations that you are inevitably going to deal with, and even if you reject them, the time and energy you spend to avoid something is a confirmation of that thing's existence. Also, remember that every position of the chart depends on others—especially the closest ones—to make sense.

The method I am introducing you to is the result of my personal research, which was grounded in some other authors' methods, but my method includes several changes and particularities. At the end of this book there is a bibliography, containing all the books that were the basis for the construction of my method.

I took the name, birth date and biography of John Lennon for this example. I chose him not only because of his great personality, but also because his life was very well documented, making it easier to confirm the aspects of the chart. Note that we must always use the full real name for the calculation. We cannot use corrected names, marriage names or nicknames. That is why we are going to use the name John Winston Lennon, instead of John Ono Lennon, the name John adopted after marrying the musician and artist Yoko Ono, or even his simplified stage name, John Lennon.

The interpretation is not personal, for we are working on the chart of a public person. That makes it impossible to go as deep into the interpretation as we would in a personal reading that is done just between the reader and the consultant. So, I will link the numbers in the chart with well-known facts of his biography, not getting into suppositions, but tracing the connection between actual facts and the chart, in order to unveil the parallels of both the human and the numerical worlds.

Esoteric Number: Represents the way the person behaves intimately—the innermost part of personality. This position reflects aspects of personality that can only be unveiled by family life.

Calculation: Add all the vowels of the full name (see figure 3 on page 24). Note that you must consider as vowels any letters that sound as vowels, and the same regarding consonants. Thus, *W* is considered a vowel in our example, because it sounds as *U*. Also, the letter *J* is consonant for "John," but a vowel for "Johann," because in "John" it sounds as *J*, a consonant; while in "Johann" it sounds as *Y*, a vowel. This means the native language of the individual must be considered.[32]

$$\begin{array}{ccccc} 6 & 5\ 9 & 6 & 5 & 6 = 37/10/1 \\ | & |\ | & | & | & | \end{array}$$

JOHN WINSTON LENNON

$$(6 + 5 + 9 + 6 + 5 + 6 = 37 \qquad 37 = 3 + 7 = 10 \qquad 1 + 0 = 1)$$

Commentary: According to what we know about number 1, we conclude that in terms of affection John was a centralized person, maybe even a bit authoritarian. Most of his biographies say that he was a typical chauvinist macho pig before marrying Yoko— who happened to be a divisor in his life. But still, even after her influence, he kept some traces of it, according to his own quotes in interviews, as well as Yoko and Sean's (their son). Observe this number 37, very positive and energetic, and meditate about how it works in a position reflecting someone's intimate relationships.

---

32. The vowels are a, e, i, o, u and sometimes w and y.

Esoteric Challenge: Challenges are the areas of life to conquer, to develop, and to accomplish in the personality. You will find different challenges throughout the chart, representing the diverse paths one must take to grow. This challenge for the inner self shows through the number what energy one is supposed to watch out for.

Calculation: Subtract the first and the last vowels of the name.

$$6 \qquad - \qquad 6 = 0$$
$$\overset{|}{\text{JOHN}} \; \text{WINSTON} \; \text{LENN}\overset{|}{\text{O}}\text{N}$$

$$(6 - 6 = 0)$$

Commentary: The challenge 0 (zero) indicates the non-existence of a particular challenge, but all of them at once. It may sound scary, but a bigger effort is expected from the ones who were gifted with better capacities.

Exoteric Number: This position shows the external "shape," your public persona, the first impression you cause; the way you behave outside your home. It is interesting to compare it with the Esoteric Number; for maybe the dichotomy is so big you cannot recognize the same person in both aspects. On the other hand, some people are kind of "transparent," presenting similar, or even the same numbers, both in esoteric and exoteric parts of the personality.

Calculation: Add the consonants of the full name.

$$1 \;\; 8 \;\; 5 \qquad 5 \;\; 1 \;\; 2 \quad 5 \quad 3 \;\; 5 \;\; 5 \qquad 5 = 45/9$$
$$\text{JOHN} \;\; \text{WINSTON} \;\; \text{LENNON}$$

$$(1 + 8 + 5 + 5 + 1 + 2 + 5 + 3 + 5 + 5 + 5 = 45 = 4 + 5 = 9)$$

Commentary: As we can see from the numbers he has, John Lennon's persona radiated, he was expansive and open. No wonder he was so popular and so daring! His tendency to defend the lower classes and minorities shows up here, for John had number 1 in his interior, which means, no matter how democratic he was in public as a result of his exoteric number 9, he was not exactly like that indoors—which does not necessarily mean that he was a hypocrite. His charisma was probably based on the fact that he dared to recognize his own weakness in public, and that gave him strength. Number 37 is a strong composition for 1, but it is not like 19—which is a number that can be benefic when placed in certain positions on the chart, but which may be difficult when in the more intimate positions, such as the Esoteric Number or the Essence. That is, he was probably demanding, but not pathologically.

Exoteric Challenge: This position exposes the decisive point in his social and professional life.

Calculation: Subtract the first and the last consonants of the full name.

$$(5 - 1 = 4)$$

Commentary: 4 is the number of bureaucracy, regular work, order, and method, all things that John disliked. This 4 also means a potential problem regarding conservatism or ceremonies. Everybody remembers the times when John caused problems for the Beatles' "good boys" public image when he was so outspoken: for example, when he declared that the band was more popular than Jesus Christ.[33]

Synthesis: This is the result of mixing the inner and outer personas; the self; the personality's big picture.

Calculation: Add all the letters of the complete name.

---

33. Marco Antonio Malagolli, *John Lennon* (São Paulo: Editora Três, 1981). Any Lennon biography will provide similar information. My source provides a complete and detailed chronology of Lennon's life and is the source for most of my research into his life.

1 6 8 5   5 9 5 1 2 6 5   3 5 5 5 6 5 = 82/10/1

JOHN WINSTON LENNON

$(1 + 6 + 8 + 5 + 5 + 9 + 5 + 1 + 2 + 6 + 5 + 3 + 5 + 5 + 5 + 6 + 5 = 82)$

$(8 + 2 = 10 \qquad 1 + 0 = 1)$

Commentary: The number 1 reinforces the genius, and explains the myth of the man. Whenever you have an addition between 9 and another number, the second will be repeated. So, Esoteric Number 1, Exoteric Number 9, and synthesis 1 is an implicit formula. Number 82, as an origin for 1, is very soft and mature, like an old soul. It confirms all the impressions that we, as audience, used to have of him, that there was great power behind the man, implicit in his work and attitude.

The General Challenge: This is the main difficulty of your personality.

Calculation: Add the previous challenges (the resulting numbers of the inner and outer challenges).

Commentary: John had a 4, since its first challenge was 0 (Esoteric Challenge, p. 67) and the second 4 (Exoteric Challenge, p. 68). That reinforces the problem with everything that 4 portrays in its symbolism.

The Path of Destiny: Represents one's life, one's path in a general way, the sky under which one walks. It is the road of existence, the way to destiny. Destiny is what you are going to find, and you have freedom of choice and can react to your destiny as you will. Your personality can predict, but not determine, this reaction. So the path of destiny is the position that unveils the kind of life you are going to have.

Calculation: Add the day, month, and year of birth.

$$10 + 9 + 1940 = 1959/24/6$$
$$(1 + 9 + 5 + 9 = 24; 2 + 4 = 6)$$

Commentary: Family, esthetics, and popularity are key words to 6. In John's case, 6 comes from 24, which is the most complicated basis for this elementary number, and the facts in his life were not what we would call easy. Regarding family, it is known that his father had left him with the mother; then the mother left little John with her sister Mimi and her husband, and the couple finally raised him. John got especially attached to his uncle, but when John was not quite a teenager, the uncle died. Also, when John was in his teens, and getting a little closer to his mother again, she got hit by a truck that was being driven by a drunken policeman. The first major period of Lennon's life is marked by different personal tragedies in the family, which is typical of the meaning of 24. But that experience also made him a humanist, a feminist and the passionate man he was. In addition, we should bear in mind that no number is a death sentence, and it may—and should—be transmuted to its higher form. I would say that John finally solved his family problem when he married Yoko, because only then he formed—after going through abortions and separation—the family he had always longed for. Number 6 brings popularity, and the worst aspect of this is that disturbed people, like John's murderer, may project all their personal failures on to a celebrity.

Choice: Shows how one exercises one's everyday life choices, and the mechanism for choosing. This position works as a complement to the synthesis number.

Calculation: Add all the letters of the first name.

$$\begin{array}{cccc} 1 & 6 & 8 & 5 \\ | & | & | & | \end{array} = 20/2$$

JOHN

Commentary: As the chart goes on, we understand better the previous positions. John was indeed a strong personality, but his choices were ruled by 2; that is, there is a clear needing to share. That adds sweetness and delicacy to his personality, which also made him vulnerable to family troubles. Not to mention that he divided his whole career into two artistic partnerships: first with Paul McCartney, with whom he composed and performed in The Beatles until the late 60s; and then with Yoko Ono, with whom John performed and composed music, directed movies, and produced art shows until his death. It was always John + 1, and not in the sense of having a shadow, since both Ono and McCartney are influential artists. John's need was to play creative games with a partner, and not to have a pupil to dominate.

Essence: This position displays what one brings inside, but not in the way we had analyzed in the Esoteric position. The Essence represents the self you do not dare to show anyone. This position is the complement to the Esoteric Number, and shows how you deal with the closest ones; while the Essence shows how you think and feel on a very intimate side. The things you know inside but do not tell, and sometimes do not even realize. It can also show what you want and what you fear the most. Note that the concepts of wish and fear are definitely linked—and this is not about sadomasochism, but about one being so scared and fixed about something that one starts wishing it would happen in order to be released from the fear of what is going to happen. Also, some people wish for something so hard that they become afraid that it won't happen.

Calculation: Add the initials, starting from the second name.

$$5 + 3 = 8$$

JOHN WINSTON LENNON

Commentary: They suggest that John was a very materialistic person in many ways. Thus, it was not surprising that he became a millionaire, even though that came from his natural talent and intuition. Besides, The Beatles had worked hard before getting famous, so it did not happen all of a sudden. This 8 indicates a concern for justice, and the fear of justice and government.

Maybe that fear made him provoke various people until he got arrested. It is all connected; just look in a good Lennon biography (see bibliography at the end of this book) and you will notice how many times he got in trouble with police and the justice system.

Balance: This position shows how one gains his or her balance. It is one's point of equilibrium, the source of harmony in everyday life. A "good" number means an easier balance, while a "bad" number indicates a lack of balance or an unusual way to find a balance.

Calculation: Add all the initials of every name.

$$1 \quad + \quad 5 \quad + \quad 3 \quad = 9$$

JOHN WINSTON LENNON

Commentary: John managed to balance himself by always moving forward, always looking for new territories to conquer. Action was better than thought. He wanted to be active and creative. Breaking external rules and crossing over the line as a way of breaking his own inner laws and frontiers was clear, since he would admit his errors, deliberately trying to unbuild the image of the idol attributed to him because of The Beatles. While he had a philosophic mind, and suggested ways of dealing with world problems, on the other hand, he retired when his son was born to be a father to his child. He even said he did not want to be taken that seriously, for a king is always killed by his vassals.

Stress Number: Represents how one reacts to outer pressures and unusual circumstances. How do you react when surprised in a new situation? The stress number indicates the quality of one's reaction.

Calculation: Add the number of Choice (see page 70) to the day of birth (October 9th).

Lennon's Choice: 20/2
Day of birth: 9
(20 + 9 = 29 = 2 + 9 = 11)

Commentary: John's expression of agility in the world was the number 11—which is Yoko Ono's number for Synthesis. Some people thought he got "nutty"—a very 11 thing to be—after they got together, but, as it usually happens with number 11, this nuttiness proved to be only an accurate vision and a strong attitude. 11 is never accepted at first, it takes some time for people to see that 11's weirdness is nothing but an ahead-of-time way of thinking. Anyway, before being the nutty Beatle, he was the "nasty"—another 11 characteristic—one, the one who behaved ironically while being decorated by the Queen. Also his fantastic lyrics, such as, "I am the Walrus," and "Lucy in the Sky with Diamonds," contain that peculiar 11s psychedelic esthetic.

Dharma: The mission, the work to do, the reason why someone is here. This is a very important position in the chart; it should be analyzed carefully. When you make the addition of who you are and how you live, you can understand what you are doing here.

Calculation: Add the number for Synthesis and the number for the Path of Destiny. Note that we must use the full original numbers, and not the final reduction, in order to get the correct results.

TABLE 1. LENNON'S DHARMA NUMBER.

Lennon's Synthesis	82
Lennon's Destiny	1959
Lennon's Dharma	2041/7

(82 + 1959 + = 2041 = 2 + 0 + 4 + 1 = 7)

Commentary: His mission was related to intellect, the understanding of mysteries, spirituality, introspection, metaphysics, and reclusion. Lennon abandoned the music business for five years after the birth of his son, Sean.

Karma: This position shows the debt or credit you may have in the chart. Let's consider karma as cause and effect, and let's see this position as a checking-of-your-mind-account. It is your conceptual inheritance.

Calculation: Add the Esoteric, Synthesis, Day of Birth, and Path of Destiny numbers, always keeping in mind that when you are adding different parts of a chart, you must use the full original numbers, otherwise you may get inaccurate results. As you become more experienced at interpreting the numbers, you will understand not only the meaning of number 8 and number 17, but also number 2087, which would be impossible if we just added the final numbers of each position.

TABLE 2. LENNON'S KARMA NUMBER.

Lennon's Esoteric Number	37
Lennon's Synthesis	82
Lennon's Day of Birth	09
Lennon's Path of Destiny	1959
Lennon's Karma	2087/17/8

$$(2 + 0 + 8 + 7 = 17 = 1 + 7 = 8)$$

Commentary: The number 8 that appeared earlier in Essence, confirms that John's feelings about wealth, justice, and the law had come from his guts, from his past, his soul. That does not involve only beautiful aspects; we should remember the many problems with the law that John had over the years. He was persecuted for a number of reasons—if not for smoking pot, for being a political subversive. Obscenity was another accusation he faced, because of the nudity on one of his album covers ("Two Virgins," one of the albums he recorded with Yoko) or in his lithographs ("Bag One") where he drowned himself and Yoko having sex. Note also that 17 is a benefic number, the number of Nuit, and of wealth.

Foundation: The foundation on which someone builds his own life and its basis.

Calculation: Just use the number of the first letter of the first name.

1   (10)

JOHN

Commentary: The number for *J* is 10, the easiest and most paternal of the 1 kind, reinforcing the importance of being a father and a leader of an era.

Power of Will: The final aim, the last card, maintaining what we started, the power of the will.

Calculation: Use the number of the last letter of the first name. Notice that when you analyze a letter you must use its "real" number, that is, the number of its position in the alphabet. For example, *A*'s value is 1, *J*'s value is 10, and *S* is 19. John, therefore, had number 14/5 for Power of Will and number 15/6 for Heart. There is a difference between someone who has only number 5 or 6, and someone who has 23/5 or 24/6. It is important to remember to use figure 3 (p. 24) when turning letters into numbers for calculation. That is, when adding letters, *A*, *J*, and *S* will always count as 1. But when analyzing the personality of a letter, you must analyze its roots; that is, its position in the alphabet, without reduction.

5   (14)

JOHN

Commentary: Number 14 shows the impetus of changing all the time, as well as a special taste for sex and drugs. It must have been hard for John to be faithful in a marriage—that is probably why he was not—as Yoko confirmed in interviews. It must also have been difficult for him to resist drugs in general.

Heart Number: The way one's sensibility speaks through; the bridge that connects with the quality of one's feelings.

Calculation: Just use the number of the first vowel of the first name.

6 (15)

JOHN

Commentary: An impulsive and passionate nature. The way to speak to his heart was to catch his sense of family, passion, and love.

The Formation of Personality: Check how many times a certain number appears in the composition of the name to understand your relationship with yourself and others, as well as your creativity, impulses and character.

Calculation: Just count how many times a certain number appears in a name, and write it in the graph. Then add the numbers vertically and horizontally for details of personality. You can use this graph when casting your own charts. Figure 6 is a blank graph that you can use for your own calculation.

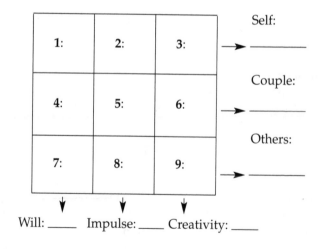

Figure 6. The name graphic.

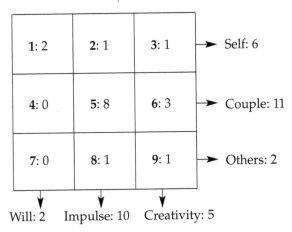

Figure 7. John Lennon's name graphic.

John had eight number 5s in his name, emphasizing his rebelliousness, his libertarianism, as well as his sexualized and ironic sides; while there are no numbers 4 or 7, which are glyphs of concentration and slowness, reflecting an impatient person (see figure 7). The number 6 is balanced, while the numbers 1, 2, 3, 8 and 9 are barely represented in the graphic. Line 1 tells us about his relationship with his own Self (box 1, 2, 3) containing four numbers (two number 1s, one number 2 and one number 3) showing that he had a good quotient of self-esteem. Still, his emotional nature was pretty confused with his self-image, which made him vulnerable to other people's feelings toward him.

The second line, marked *Couple* (box 4, 5, 6), reflects the relationships in our minds. Lennon had 11 as his Couple number, which indicates why he abandoned the Beatles when he fell in love with Yoko: for John, to have a partner was essential, and he used to say that Yoko was like a friend with whom he had sex, so he felt completed. He did not really care about The Beatles' public matters, as you can tell because he only had two numbers on line 3 (box 7, 8, 9) for Others. His way to achieve spiritual and emotional fulfillment—his personal path to transcendence—was to share everything with one person, not with everybody, even though he was concerned about community affairs, which is the number 9 part of his personality. Creativity (column 3) has a medium representation (five numbers), which is also the number for change and evolution. It suggests that his creations came from his guts rather than from his brain.

There was a lot of impulsiveness in his personality (see column 2), and his will (column 1), depending on the partner, would be weak or strong. He needed to rely on someone to be as brilliant as he was.

Subconscious: This position shows one's irrational reactions.

Calculation: Subtract the number of missing numbers in the Formation of Personality from 9.

> Lennon's absent numbers: 2
> (9 - 2 = 7)

Commentary: Number 7, when reflecting the subconscious, suggests a person who tends toward isolation (one of Lennon's songs is titled "Isolation") and self-criticism. This was his natural defense.

Heredity: Here we analyze the inheritance, the family name.

Calculation: Add all the letters of the last name (the surname) individually.

$$3\;5\;5\;\;5\;\;6\;\;5 = 29/11$$

LENNON

$$(3 + 5 + 5 + 5 + 6 + 5 = 29 = 2 + 9 = 11)$$

Commentary: One more number 11 in his map, confirming the genius and the visionary, as well as the eccentric. I am not familiar with his father's biography, but the echoes of a male role in his chart suggest that John's sarcasm came from his father.

The Second Name: This is just the analysis of a middle name or second name, if there is one. In John's case, his middle name was Winston, for this was not a "family" name.

Calculation: Add all the letters in the name(s).

$$5\ 9\ 5\ 1\ 2\ 6\ 5 = 33/6$$

WINSTON

$$(5 + 9 + 5 + 1 + 2 + 6 + 5 = 33 = 3 + 3 = 6)$$

Commentary: This name emphasizes all Lennon's sentimental traces, the need for a family to support him emotionally, and the need for self-expression.

Professional Advice: In this position we can appreciate one's professional talents.

Calculation: Just analyze and compare the numbers of Day of Birth, Synthesis, Path of Destiny, Dharma and Karma to get an idea of various professions that would be more appropriate for the individual. The more a certain activity is represented by a number, the more it is the symbol of the right profession. To interpret the relationship between numbers and profession, you can use Table 3 on page 80. Lennon's numbers are as follows:

> Day of Birth: 9
> Synthesis (see p. 68): 82/10/1
> Path of Destiny (see p. 69); 1959/24/6
> Dharma (see p. 73): 2041/7
> Karma (see p. 74): 2087/17/8

Table 3. Numbers and Professions.

1 Leader, Boss, Spokesman, Pilot, Commander, Politician, Inventor, Publicity, Education, Sales, Manager; good dealing with collaborators, but only plays the role of the leader who designates tasks.
2 Musician, Mathematician, Painter, Dancer, Statistic, Bookkeeper, Numerologist, Astrologer, Systems Analyst, Writer, Physician, Diplomat, Public Service, Cooperator; works better in a partnership.
3 Artist, Communicator, Journalist, Speaker, Lawyer; Aesthetician, Creator, Sociologist, Designer; good dealing with children.
4 Farmer, Agriculturist, Geologist, Military, Constructor, Architect, Engineer, Administrator, Archivist, Librarian, Mechanic, Sculptor, Politician, Demolisher, Realtor; good with hierarchies and bureaucracy.
5 Mannequin, Board Commissary, Stylist, Tourist Guide, Importer/Exporter, Pilot, Businessperson, Psychologist, Sports, Sexologist, Chemist, Dealer; good for fashion, vanities, travels, and adventures.
6 Doctor, Nurse, Artist, Cook, Social affairs, Veterinary, Botanic, Decoration, Assistant, Community, Musicology; good with communities, children, and seniors.
7 Researcher, Philosopher, Historian, Occultist, Archeologist, Museum staff, Writer, Psychologist, Homeopathy, Alternative therapies, Professor, Scientist, Artist, Parapsychology; works well alone, using thought and concentration.
8 Economist, Lawyer, Judge, Manager, Banker, Dealer, Industry, Conductor; works related to Minerals, Diplomat, Entertainer; works well with big companies and conglomerates.
9 Artist, Actor, Decorator, Tourist Guide, Board commissary, Import/Export, Social matters, Spokesperson, Occultist, Doctor, Politician, Sports; works well with images, and deals well with big crowds.
11 Artist (avant-garde), Philosopher, Systems Analyst, Occultist, Inventor, Chemist; unusual works in general.
22 Diplomat, Humanist, Manager, Agent, Boss, Industrial, Imports/Exports, Education, Constructor, Writer, Missionary; works well with causes related to humanity or the planet.

Commentary: Lennon had combinations of 9, 1, 6, 7 and 8. His artistic talent appears in 9, 6 and 7. By the way, 6 is more musical, while 9 is linked with crowds, and 7 with intellect. Lennon actually was the "intellectual" Beatle, so to speak. He wrote two books, and was also an artist (he produced lithographs, drawings, etc.); he was also a filmmaker (he shot some film with Yoko as well as by himself), and an actor (he was in all the Beatles movies, as well as in a movie called "How I Won the War"). The leader appears in numbers 1 and 8.

Sexuality: Everyone wants to know about the nature and quality of the manifestation of his or her sexuality.

Calculation: Compare the numbers of Esoteric, Essence, Synthesis, Dharma and Path of Destiny, using Table 4 (p. 82) for suggestions on the correlation between sex and numbers: Lennon's numbers are as follows:

> Esoteric (see p. 66): 37/10/1
> Essence (see p. 71): 8
> Synthesis (see p. 68): 82/10/1
> Dharma (see p. 73): 2041/7
> Path of Destiny (see p. 69): 1959/24/6

Commentary: John had numbers 1, 8, 1, 7, 6. He was mainly active, dominant, creative, daring. And his sexuality was evident in his career—I refer you to his "Two Virgins" album, famous for displaying the naked bodies of Yoko and John, front and back; or his erotic lithograph "Bag One," or his movie "Self-Portrait," which was a long shot of his erect penis. The procreative factor of 6 is also confirmed since he was a father pretty early—he married Cynthia Powell because she was pregnant with his first son, Julian.

TABLE 4. NUMBERS AND SEX.

1 Aggressive sexuality, domination, intensity; an egocentric lover who must be admired.
2 Delicacy, affection, passiveness, mysterious, shy, ambiguity; a romantic and sometimes concealed sexuality.
3 Theatrical sexuality; plays games, inventive; sex is a source of happiness and fantasy; an infantile personality includes an immature sexuality, which may manifest as being coy or pathological.
4 Sometimes a devastatingly intense sexuality; sometimes blocked desire; violence and sensitivity; traditional; represses crude instincts.
5 Intense sexuality, more physical than affective; fantasies are a must; needs to experiment; a fearless lover; raving and inconsequential, walking the path of excess to find pleasure.
6 Affectionate, sex for reproduction, love. Family is the manifestation of sex; compromise and pact as the antechamber of the Garden of Eros.
7 Self-eroticism; masturbation; attraction related to the intellect, both in the sense that the person gets excited over another's intelligence, as well as being a person who conceptualizes sexuality, living out hidden fantasies. Coldness.
8 A sexual volcano; looks subtle, but may be scandalous. Passionate; exaggerates; sex is linked to power, especially to material power. Not only an opportunistic lover, but also one who gets turned on by powerful people, not because of money itself, but what it represents in power and influence.
9 Anxiety, inventiveness, experimentation; sex may be used as an outlet for anxiety, which may be constructive or not, depending on the circumstances. Some people cannot be loyal to one person, so monogamy may not be for this number.
11 Ambiguity; androgyny; originality; unconventional; exotic fantasies, magick, tantra; sex as the Highest Sacrament or the lower vice, both following a path beyond polarity.
22 Shyness hides intensity; out of control. Intense sexuality may be experimental or perverted—and perversion is a cultural concept, which changes dramatically from culture to culture.

Basic Challenge: As the very name says, this is the main challenge of one's life.

Calculation: Subtract the numbers of the day of birth. People who are born on the 1, 2, 3, 4, 5, 6, 7, 8, 9, 11, or 22 of any month will have 0 has the Basic Challenge. (You can't subtract single digit numbers, and 1 - 1 = 0; 2 - 2 = 0. However, if you were born on the 27th, 7 - 2 = 5.)

Lennon's day of birth = 09

Commentary: No basic obstruction. John's main problems were really about family.

Basic Credit: The name says it all. This number is the lucky star, the good thing in one's life.

Calculation: Subtract the Basic Challenge from 9.

Commentary: Since John had no Challenge, he had no special Credit. Usually, the Credit is a weapon against the Challenge.

First Challenge: This is a challenge for the first half of one's life. It is difficult to determine when it ends, since we never know how long we are going to live.

Calculation: Subtract the day and the month of birth. Obviously you will always subtract the smaller number from the larger number.

Lennon's day of birth: 09
Lennon's month of birth: 10
(9 - 1 = 8)

Commentary: John's main difficulty until his 20s—half of his short lifetime—was about money.

Second Challenge: The challenge for the second half of one's life.

Calculation: Subtract the month and the year of birth.

Lennon's month of birth: 10
Lennon's year of birth: 14 (1940)
(14 - 1 = 13/4)

Commentary: Adaptation problems, repression, and loss. It is probably about the miscarriages that happened when he and Yoko were trying to have a baby. They only succeeded in giving birth to Sean, who was already their fourth attempt to have a baby. Also, it may be an indication of the pressure of the world on his shoulders, first because of the paranoia caused by The Beatles' incomparable success; and then because of the process of confronting the previous concepts the public had on him with his actual being. Even though he was one of the more malicious of the Beatles, he had to deconstruct his good-Beatle-boy image to let John Lennon, the Working Class Hero—who officially renamed himself John Ono Lennon—arise.

The Karmic Challenge: As the very name says, the most important challenge to take.

Calculation: Subtract the First and the Second Challenges (see pp. 83–84).

> Lennon's First Challenge: 8
> Lennon's Second Challenge: 13
> (13 - 8 = 5)

Commentary: His biggest challenges were to take control of drugs, and to balance his creative enthusiasm with his impatience. Drugs were a big problem for John, especially alcohol and heroin. Some of the psychedelic drugs inspired him to write some of his classics. And moving was a big challenge, since he had to face a long process of getting permission to stay in the United States at the time when his so-called subversive political activities were not considered sympathetically by the Nixon government. He went through a lot until he got his green card—after Nixon's fall.

The Life–Cycles and Pinnacles: This section describes a combination of cycles and pinnacles, which are all associated with the Path of Destiny. There are major Life Cycles, which we will look at separately. Pinnacles are representative of the seasons and describes four major times of change in your life.

Cycles: These are actually Subpaths of Destiny, divided into three portions of time. They unveil the influences coming from deep inside; they relate to intimate matters.

Calculation: There are three major life cycles. The first cycle starts at birth and changes around age 28 (this age will vary based on your month of birth as we will explain shortly). The 2nd cycle runs from age 28 or so until age 56 (28 years later). The 3rd cycle starts around age 56 and astrologers feel we start another around the ages of 84–86. Calculation of these cycles is a bit intricate; so let's divide it into parts.

The **1st cycle** begins at birth and ends around your Personal Year 1 closest to age 28—a number that is mathematically perfect, representing the end of an archetypal cycle. First, calculate your personal annual numbers, the numbers that rule each year of your life. This calculation involves adding the month and day of birth, to the particular year you want to explore. When you do this, you will note that the Personal Year number follows a cycle; that is, after Personal Year number 1 comes number 2 or 11, then the 3, then the 4 or 22, then 5, and so on, until you reach 9. After 9, the Personal Year number will be 1 again, restarting the cycle. Thus you need to find the Personal Year number 1 closest to age 28. This will mark the end of the 1st cycle and the beginning of the 2nd. Please look at Table 5 (page 86) for a sample based on Lennon's chart. You'll see that Lennon was a slow cycler and did not move into his 2nd cycle until age 31. Also note that the year between the end of a cycle and the beginning of another is a transition period. The two numbers mix their vibrations, for one is decreasing and the other is increasing. In other words, the year overlaps and the two cycles (the one ending and the one beginning) also overlap.

TABLE 5. DETERMINING LENNON'S PERSONAL YEAR.*

YEAR	PERSONAL YEAR NO.	AGE
1962	1	22 years old
1963	2	23 years old
1964	3	24 years old
1965	22	25 years old
1966	5	26 years old
1967	6	27 years old
1968	7	28 years old
1969	8	29 years old
1970	9	30 years old
1971	1	31 years old

As you see, number 28 marks a median age of transition, but the personal date of transition for Lennon is marked by the Personal Annual Number 1 that is closest to this general age. Thus, 31 years of age is the frontier between the 1st and the 2nd cycles in Lennon's chart. He will remain in his 1st cycle until he is 31.

2nd Cycle: The number of the day of birth is used to calculate the 2nd cycle, which begins during the end of the 1st cycle. Actually, the year that marks the end of a cycle and the beginning of the next one is always a mixed period, for it combines the vibrations attached to the numbers for both the 1st and 2nd cycles. That principle will apply to every cycle and pinnacle. The 2nd cycle, in turn, ends around the Personal Annual Year 1 closest to age 56. So we add 1940 and 56[34] to obtain 1996 (the year John would complete 56 years of life). Now we add 1996 plus 9 (day) plus 10 (month). The result is 2015/8: Lennon's Personal Year for 1996. Again, we must find the year closest to a Personal Number 1. So we go two steps forward (see Table 5, page 86) to find the Personal Number 2017/10/1, by adding 1998 + 10 + 9, which would be

---

*To build your own table, calculate your number for age 28. Then add or subtract by 1 until you create a list like the one above. Keep going until you have two "1" years to choose from. Your second cycle will be starting the year closest to age 28.

34. Note that 28 x 2 = 56. This is a Saturn relationship, Saturn being tied to "Father Time," and being associated with life and death in astrological symbolism and cycles.

at Lennon's 58th birthday, marking the end of the 2nd cycle and beginning of the 3rd. See Table 6 (page 88) for our calculations. Again, he is not changing cycles at the average age, but a couple of years later.

3rd Cycle: Its number is the same as the year of birth: 1940 = 5. It begins during the end of the previous cycle, and it ends with Lennon's death. We need no calculation at all. The fact that Lennon did not live out this cycle, as well as the last pinnacle, does not mean the chart is not efficient, as a radical rationalist mind might think. The aim of the present study is not to divine one's death. Not even the most modern medicine has succeeded in these matters. Some mysteries must be maintained, or discovered in other ways, or at another time.

So, the final result of the calculation of the cycles goes like this:

1st Cycle = 10/1 (from 0 to 31 years of age)
2nd Cycle = 09 (from 31 to 58 years of age)
3rd Cycle = 14/5 (from 58 and forward)

Pinnacles: There are four pinnacles, and they represent the four seasons and their corresponding numbers. You can gather information regarding external facts by using the pinnacles.

Calculation: Just like the cycles, we must go step by step to learn the calculation for the pinnacles.

1st Pinnacle: *Spring* (our start in life)—For the number of the pinnacle, add the day and the month of birth, in John's case, 9 (day) + 10 (month) = 19/1. Subtract the Path of Destiny number (in John's case, 6) from 36. (The cycle of man = 9 and four cycles = 9 x 4 = 36; this is always the number used to create the 1st pinnacle.) So, 36 - 6 (John's Path of Destiny), tells us that age 30 is when John's 1st pinnacle ends. There is a period of a year when the vibration of the cycle that is ending and the cycle that's starting mix. The same is valid for pinnacles. This kind of vibration does not start or end immediately; it actually fades and rises gradually. This period lasts for a year and marks the decrease of the old cycle and the increase of the new one.

TABLE 6. LENNON'S 2ND CYCLE ENDS.

YEAR	PERSONAL YEAR NO.	AGE
<u>1989</u>	<u>1</u>	<u>49</u>
1990	2	50
1991	3	51
1992	4	52
1993	5	53
1994	6	54
1995	7	55
<u>1996</u>	<u>8</u>	<u>56</u>
1997	9	57
<u>1998</u>	<u>1</u>	<u>58</u>

2nd Pinnacle: *Summer* (our obligations)—This number is determined by adding the day and year of birth. Its symbolism lasts for nine years. So, for John we add 9 + 1940 = 1949/23/5; thus the 2nd pinnacle begins at age 31 and ends when he is 40 years old. The number 5 will be important to him for 9 years.

3rd Pinnacle: *Autumn* (the great prophetic indicator)—Add the 1st and the 2nd pinnacles to obtain the number for the 3rd pinnacle, which also lasts for nine years. In John's case, we add 1949 + 19 = 1968/24/6, so the 3rd pinnacle lasts from his 39th through his 48th year, during which time the number 6 is important to him.

4th Pinnacle: *Winter* (wisdom)—Add the month and the year of birth (1940 + 10 = 1950 = 15 = 6). This cycle begins during the end of the previous pinnacle, and goes forward. So from age 49 onward, he is involved with number 6. The result is the following:

> 1st Pinnacle = 19/1 (from age 0 to 30);
> 2nd Pinnacle = 23/5 (from age 30 to 39);
> 3rd Pinnacle = 1968/24/6 (from age 39 to 48);
> 4th Pinnacle = 1950/15/6 (from age 48 forward).

Now, we must bring together the cycles, pinnacles and the Path of Destiny, turning the three of them into periods. In order to do so, we can approximate the dates, but only when the difference is no more than one year. That is, if the cycle ends at age 28, and the pinnacle ends at age 29, we can approximate it as a period ending at age 29, for example. The transition of the numerical vibration is not rigid; it takes about a year. Still, we should give preference to the pinnacle, since this is a shorter time period than a cycle. Let's look at an example:

1st Period—Path 24/6—Cycle 10/1—Pinnacle 19/1 (from 0 to 30);

2nd Period—Path 24/6—Cycle 9—Pinnacle 23/5 (from 30 to 39);

3rd Period—Path 24/6—Cycle 9—Pinnacle 24/6 (from 39 to 48);

4th Period—Path 24/6—Cycle 9—Pinnacle 15/6 (from 48 to 58);

5th Period—Path 24/6—Cycle 14/5—Pinnacle 15/6 (from 58 forward).

Commentary: John's 1st period brought the combination of 24/6, 10/1 and 19/1. The conjunction of two 1s (especially one of them being a 19) is kind of tough and arrogant, qualities that John definitely loved to demonstrate during his first thirty years of life. Of course, the combination emphasizes the exceptional leader that he was, and also some egoism, but you can only understand it all under the perspective of the 24/6, for it covers both the 10 and the 19, showing that all the arrogance and subtle violence he demonstrated was actually a cry for help as well as his defense. That particular conjunction suggests negligence regarding family matters. John's first marriage took place only because of Cynthia's pregnancy. Julian, his first son, was born in the beginning of the Beatles hysteria, which made the parents distant from each other because of the activity in the group. And we can also see the transition from Cynthia to Yoko, and the negative reaction from the outer world (19) toward his second marriage, but transmuted into Peace Happenings, linked to the 10 in the cycle.

His 2nd period mixes 24/6, 9, and 23/5—an explosive combination—for 9 and 5 are inflamed numbers, libertarian, daring, bold. In that period Lennon manifested his mordacity more than ever. He was involved with radical activists and his art was censored. Also his telephone calls were recorded by the authorities, who wanted to deport him. And when 5 meets 6, it is not exactly an harmonic meeting, for they are not compatible. Indeed, Lennon had problems in his relationship with Yoko, and was separated from her for eighteen months, but the number 6 in the path is bigger, and symbolizes the permanent link, the coming back. That is so because, since the Path of Destiny provides the music for life's song, his choice would always be to give preference to family, whether good or bad. But don't misunderstand it, and think that it was his "destiny." It was the *tendency* of the *nature* of his life that made him choose so. And, when one has the knowledge of one's tendencies, one has the chance to *control it* — not in a pretentious rational way, but rather as a depuration of the will upon anything that distracts it. This is what the chart and this book are all about.

The combination of two moving numbers, such as 5 and 9, suggests travel. There was a great deal of travel on tours with The Beatles during the previous period, so that was not new for him in the 2nd period. The difference was the peculiar conjunction of facts: Lennon had moved from his native country, England; had married a foreigner; and raised his son with her in the most multicultural city in the world, New York. So, there was a little bit more than just travel in the connection, but 6 (marriage, family), 5 (challenge, moving, unpredictability), and 9 (internationality, communication, big masses), are all creative numbers.

In addition, the drugs were an absolute reality, as well as his healing from that through macrobiotics—6 for cure (and for sickness), 5 and 9 for sex, drugs and rock'n'roll.[35] And 9 is a symbol of amplitude, and that can force a couple apart, sometimes, because there is no more intimacy, everything is too plentiful, too spacious, and it gets even bigger. But it seems that this was a particularly happy period in the end, probably because John and Yoko learned how to deal with the energy that surrounded them.

---

35. The circumstances make it inevitable to use this expression.

The birth of Sean grounded them and John was stable with Yoko, maybe because he used to travel and discover new things with Sean while Yoko was working to multiply their wealth and properties. He was dealing with the peculiar tendencies of 5 and 9 that insinuate controversy as well as discovering new sensations, both channeled toward family (6) and healing (24). John decided to take care of Sean, in order not to incur the same error he had made with Julian, and that his mother and father had made with himself. The retirement to raise Sean was his way of breaking the chain that attached him to a pattern of sorrow.

The 3rd period was barely lived, for John was unfortunately murdered at age 40, and the period begins at 39. However, the brief sample of this 3rd period was a transition from five reclusive years raising his son to the new beginning with a new album with Yoko, called *Double Fantasy*. It is weird that the conjunction is 24/6, 9, for 24/6 suggests an emotional battle, struggle, and suffering. We never know nature's reasons and what really happens in the intricate web of life. Also, my aim with this book and this chart is not to judge things, but to analyze them. The combination suggests a familiar drama, and I am not sure if it was a sign of the bitter fact that he was killed exactly when he was feeling more accomplished; or if there was something bad for him to face later that he did not experience because he was not here. Or maybe he would have channeled the energy of those numbers, just like he seemed to have done in the period before.

Obviously, we cannot interpret the following periods, since Lennon died and it would be waste of time to build empty theories to see if they match history.

The Tarot Arcana: There is a correspondence between numbers and arcana of the tarot, which also provides a panoramic view of the individual.

Calculation: Add the numbers of each name separately. Add the names once more (excluding elementary and master numbers). Then, add the result of the names, and the final result is the number of the Arcana. Then find it in Table 7 (p. 92).

TABLE 7. NUMBERS AND THE MAJOR ARCANA IN THE THOTH DECK.

NUMBER	CARD	CHARACTERISTICS OF THE MAJOR ARCANA
1	THE MAGUS	Wisdom, sense of opportunity, flexibility, communicability, talent, the top.
2	THE PRIESTESS	Intuition, esoteric knowledge, receptivity, inner equilibrium, the veil of Isis.
3	THE EMPRESS	Love, beauty, delicacy, elegance, happiness, procreation, sensuality.
4	THE EMPEROR	Conquering, leadership, pioneer, activity, stability, megalomania.
5	THE HIEROPHANT	Divine knowledge, master, spirituality, persistency, manipulation.
6	THE LOVERS	Love, attraction, doubt, indecision, unity of opposites, choice to make.
7	THE CHARIOT	Victory, triumph, to go, introspection, planning, health, new beginnings.
8	ADJUSTMENT	Justice, stability, equilibrium, law, concentration, balance.
9	THE HERMIT	Interior, illumination, prudence, wisdom, end of cycle, self-knowledge.
10	FORTUNE	Change, new beginnings, destiny, sudden happenings, expansion, growing.
11	LUST	Vital force, passion, energy, courage, domain, magick powers, reason/instinct.
12	THE HANGED MAN	Sacrifice, redemption, stagnation, end of an impasse, giving up, victimization, understanding.
13	DEATH	Transformation, liberation, death and rebirth, radicalism, outer change.
14	ART	Unification of opposite polarities, inner change, alchemy, creativity, realization.
15	THE DEVIL	Vitality, material possessions, passion, sex, impulsiveness, sense of humor, desire, greed.
16	THE TOWER	Destruction, radical and painful transformation, end of something, renovation, obstacles, courage, self-criticism.

TABLE 7. NUMBERS AND THE MAJOR ARCANA IN THE THOTH DECK. (CONT.)

NUMBER	CARD	CHARACTERISTICS OF THE MAJOR ARCANA
17	THE STAR	Hope, reconnection with the best energies inside, clarity, illumination, light at the end of the tunnel, naïveté.
18	THE MOON	Unconscious, fear, illusion, the unknown, intuition, craziness, a new level of consciousness.
19	THE SUN	Accomplishment, spirituality, charisma, success, wealth, glory, fame, arrogance, vanity.
20	THE AEON	Separation of past and future, analysis of past errors, deep change of value, change of point of view and of mind.
21	THE WORLD	Synthesis, end of problems, unification, development, universality, internationality, perseverance.
22	THE FOOL	Absence of time and space, freedom, independence, inner voice, channeling, craziness, exoticism, ideas.

$$1\ 6\ \ 8\ 5 \qquad 5\ 9\ 5\ 1\ 2\ 6\ 5 \qquad 3\ 5\ 5\ 5\ 6\ 5$$

JOHN WINSTON LENNON

$$20 \qquad\quad 33 \qquad\quad 29$$
$$2\ \ +\ \ 6\ \ +\ \ 11\ \ =\ \ 19:\quad \text{The Sun}$$

John's major arcana card from the tarot deck is The Sun, representing creativity, passionate love, luminosity, success, and male energy. There are lots of different tarot packs; some of them are really good ones, like the Mythological Tarot, the Marseilles Tarot (the so-called "classic" pack), the Papus Bohemian Tarot, the Merlin Tarot, and others. Each deck follows different numeric and symbolic systems, even though they are based on similar sources, showing different points of view on a subject. Choosing a tarot deck is as intimate as choosing the person with whom you are going to make love. Maybe even more. However, since it is that intimate, there is no rule, no good or bad about it. I choose to use the Thoth Tarot, designed by Aleister Crowley and Frieda Harris, because I think it is connected to our modern times; it's very beautiful and impressive, and the drawings contain much more information than any other deck I ever saw. Therefore, Table 7 (p. 93) is good for the Thoth Tarot. But if you use another pack, just put the major arcana in order (that order varies from deck to deck) and associate the resulting number with the arcana, and what you know about the arcana itself.

I am not able to agree with the popular linking of the major arcana card for Justice (or Adjustment) with the number 11, and the major arcana for Force (or Lust) with the number 8, because in terms of number symbolism it just does not fit for me. Since number symbolism came before everything, as a concept, and before any tarot arcana, I think the connection is obviously 11 for Power/Lust and 8 for Justice/Adjustment. Students of the tarot will want to think about this.

If you are associated with a minor arcana card, you should also analyze the major arcana. If you are a number 29, you have two arcanae to analyze: the 3 of Wands and Lust (11). See Table 8, pages 94–97 for a breakdown of what these cards mean.

Life Path: This is a conjunction of letters and numbers. This position provides the most specific information about temporary vibrations that are passing through your life. Every number or letter in the graph is a relevant sign, but the "conjunctions "are the real thing in terms of what really matters on this graph. Conjunctions occur when every number and/or letter happens at the same time, and they can happen for bad or for good; it depends on one's capacity for adaptation. Usually the numbers appear more than once, like a repetitive pattern, even though they don't materialize every time they occur. Most of the time, if a conjunction is strong the first time—that is, if its manifestation is clear—it becomes weaker and weaker when it returns; and if it does not manifest itself in the beginning, probably the second coming will be stronger. Let's look at how we build the Life Path, step by step:

TABLE 8. NUMBERS AND THE MINOR ARCANA IN THE THOTH DECK.

NUMBER	CARD	CHARACTERISTICS OF THE MINOR ARCANA
23	KNIGHT OF WANDS	Fire and fire, activity, generosity, impetuosity, sometimes aggressiveness, changing, evolution.
24	QUEEN OF WANDS	Water and fire, generosity and impatience, compassion, self-knowledge, attraction, veiled domain.
25	PRINCE OF WANDS	Air and fire, burning love, intensity, delicacy and roughness combined, sense of humor, creativity.
26	PRINCESS OF WANDS	Earth and fire, domain, resumption, fearlessness, exaggeration, brightness, optimism, destruction of fears.
27	ACE OF WANDS	Great energy for development, will.
28	TWO OF WANDS	Confrontation with equivalent powers, influence.
29	THREE OF WANDS	Virtue, integrity, realization, stability through movement.
30	FOUR OF WANDS	Effort, work, recompense for perseverance.
31	FIVE OF WANDS	Fighting, competition, violence, restriction, obstacles that overwhelm.
32	SIX OF WANDS	Victory, love, success, satisfaction.
33	SEVEN OF WANDS	Valor, courage, integrity, no concessions, confrontation.
34	EIGHT OF WANDS	Agility, quickness, clear and objective communication, a message.
35	NINE OF WANDS	Power, health, surpassing obstacles, totality.
36	TEN OF WANDS	Oppression, block, impasse, aggression, repression.
37	KNIGHT OF CUPS	Fire and water, giving, love, immaturity, drugs, instability.
38	QUEEN OF CUPS	Water and water, maternity, poetry, cloudy expression.
39	PRINCE OF CUPS	Air and water, anxiety, subterfuge, apparent calmness, hidden violence, transformation, sex, secret wishes.

TABLE 8. NUMBERS AND THE MINOR ARCANA IN THE THOTH DECK. (CONT.)

NUMBER	CARD	CHARACTERISTICS OF THE MINOR ARCANA
40	PRINCESS OF CUPS	Earth and water, self-confidence, emotional freedom, grace, sensuality, romanticism, self-indulgence.
41	ACE OF CUPS	Overflowing love, clarity, the seed of love (both literally and subjectively).
42	TWO OF CUPS	Love, receptiveness, marriage, the tasty side of love.
43	THREE OF CUPS	Abundance, sensuality, hospitality, pleasure, relaxing, ecstasy.
44	FOUR OF CUPS	Exuberance, love, out of control, insecure, jealous, good beginning/bad ending, waste of love.
45	FIVE OF CUPS	Deception, frustration, unrealized hopes, problematic relationships.
46	SIX OF CUPS	Pleasure, desire, sexuality, renovation, pre-tension, extension, light.
47	SEVEN OF CUPS	Licentiousness, promiscuity, intoxication, illusion.
48	EIGHT OF CUPS	Indolence, laziness, stagnation, unstable success.
49	NINE OF CUPS	Happiness, luck, health, self-indulgence, fun.
50	TEN OF CUPS	Satiety, plenitude, accommodation.
51	KNIGHT OF SWORDS	Fire and air, firmness, persistence, plans, schemes, intellectualism, dynamism.
52	QUEEN OF SWORDS	Water and air, objectivity, rationality, logic, vengeance, breaking conventions.
53	PRINCE OF SWORDS	Air and air, intuition, philosophy, great vision, creative thought, mental domain.
54	PRINCESS OF SWORDS	Earth and air, fighting, faithfulness, rebellion, anger, cut, reaction.
55	ACE OF SWORDS	Brilliant thought, good idea, elaboration, inspiration, a contact with entity or being.
56	TWO OF SWORDS	Temporary peace, accord, tranquillity, balanced decisions.

TABLE 8. NUMBERS AND THE MINOR ARCANA IN THE THOTH DECK. (CONT.)

NUMBER	CARD	CHARACTERISTICS OF THE MINOR ARCANA
57	THREE OF SWORDS	Pain, separation, interference, decision, mixed thoughts.
58	FOUR OF SWORDS	Truce, centralization, growing, relaxing after trouble.
59	FIVE OF SWORDS	Defeat, fear of defeat, insecurity, malice, unknown fear.
60	SIX OF SWORDS	Science, analysis, mental coordination, comprehension, success after anxiety, intelligence.
61	SEVEN OF SWORDS	Frivolity, exhaustion, despondency, futility, to dazzle, baseless fears.
62	EIGHT OF SWORDS	Interference, indetermination, too much concentration on details, lack of objectivity.
63	NINE OF SWORDS	Cruelty, mental agony, torture, preoccupation, malice, hopelessness, self-punishment, victimization, martyrdom, fanaticism.
64	TEN OF SWORDS	Ruin, death, failure, bad thoughts, sadness, accumulation of negative vibrations.
65	KNIGHT OF DISKS	Fire and earth, cure, doctor, result of efforts, work to do, jealousy.
66	QUEEN OF DISKS	Water and earth, fertility, fecundity, practicality, transformation of adverse conditions.
67	PRINCE OF DISKS	Air and earth, control, management, competency, prevention, prudence, matter.
68	PRINCESS OF DISKS	Earth and earth, pregnancy, being reborn, stability, continuity.
69	ACE OF DISKS	Wealth, richness, beginning, unification of body and soul.
70	TWO OF DISKS	Change, vital cycle, transformation, ups and downs, equilibrium, association.
71	THREE OF DISKS	Work, business, development, self-confidence.
72	FOUR OF DISKS	Power, integrity, seriousness, rigor.

Table 8. Numbers and the Minor Arcana in the Thoth Deck. (cont.)

NUMBER	CARD	CHARACTERISTICS OF THE MINOR ARCANA
73	FIVE OF DISKS	Preoccupation, archetypal fears, tension, incomprehension, intelligence, transformation.
74	SIX OF DISKS	Success, luck, acceptance, giving, a gift, chance.
75	SEVEN OF DISKS	Failure, fear of failure, small obstacles that look enormous, resignation, accommodation, cynicism, deception.
76	EIGHT OF DISKS	Prudence, to beware, prevention, knowledge.
77	NINE OF DISKS	Gain, wealth, richness, triangle.
78	TEN OF DISKS	Richness, prosperity, abundance.

1. Take note the date of birth (day, month, year) and its evolution, day by day (John Lennon was born on October 9, 1940).

2. Do the same with the corresponding age at every birthday. In Table 9 (pp. 100–101), you'll see a list of birth month, day, and year, followed by Lennon's age 0–40. (You could pick another age, such as 84, if you wanted to make a thorough Life Path graph.) In the column "Transit," you'll see *JWL* (John Winston Lennon). The "Essence" for the year is 9. (To create your own Essence number, see page 71; add your initials.)

3. Take note of the transit of letters in the transit column on Table 9. To do this, you write down the letters of the first name in the first column. In the second column, write down the letters of the second name. In the third column, write down the letters of the last name. Each letter remains in the graph for the number of years that correspond to the number that rules the letter. For example: *C* will remain for three years, *I* will last for 9 years, *A* for 1 year. To understand this clearly, you must learn the number value of all the letters.

TABLE 9. JOHN WINSTON LENNON'S LIFE PATH.

DATE	AGE	TRANSIT	ESSENCE	PERSONAL YEAR
10.9.1940	00	J W L	9	24/6
10.9.1941	01	O W L	14/5	16/7
10.9.1942	02	O W L	14/5	17/8
10.9.1943	03	O W E	16/7	18/9
10.9.1944	04	O W E	16/7	19/1
10.9.1945	05	O I E	20/2	20/2
10.9.1946	06	O I E	20/2	21/3
10.9.1947	07	H I E	22	22
10.9.1948	08	H I N	22	23/5
10.9.1949	09	H I N	22	24/6
10.9.1950	10	H I N	22	25/7
10.9.1951	11	H I N	22	17/8
10.9.1952	12	H I N	22	18/9
10.9.1953	13	H I N	22	19/1
10.9.1954	14	H N N	18/9	20/2
10.9.1955	15	N N N	15/6	21/3
10.9.1956	16	N N N	15/6	22
10.9.1957	17	N N N	15/6	23/5
10.9.1958	18	N N O	16/7	24/6
10.9.1959	19	N S O	12/3	25/7
10.9.1960	20	J T O	9	26/8
10.9.1961	21	O T O	14/5	18/9
10.9.1962	22	O O O	18/9	19/1
10.9.1963	23	O O O	18/9	20/2
10.9.1964	24	O O N	17/8	21/3
10.9.1965	25	O O N	17/8	22
10.9.1966	26	O O N	17/8	23/5
10.9.1967	27	H O N	19/1	24/6
10.9.1968	28	H N N	18/9	25/6
10.9.1969	29	H N L	16/7	26/8
10.9.1970	30	H N L	16/7	27/9
10.9.1971	31	H N L	16/7	19/1
10.9.1972	32	H N E	18/9	20/2
10.9.1973	33	H W E	18/9	21/3
10.9.1974	34	H W E	18/9	22
10.9.1975	35	N W E	15/6	23/5
10.9.1976	36	N W E	15/6	24/6
10.9.1977	37	N W N	15/6	25/7
10.9.1978	38	N I N	19/1	26/8
10.9.1979	39	N I N	19/1	27/9
10.9.1980	40	J I N	15/6	28/1

1	2	3	4	5	6	7	8	9
A	B	C	D	E	F	G	H	I
J	K	L	M	N	O	P	Q	R
S	T	U	V	W	X	Y	Z	

John Lennon was born October 9, 1940.

4. Observe where the letter is, and if it is placed in the first column (at the physical level); in the second column (at the emotional level) or in the third column (at the spiritual level). A person who has more than three names accumulates two or more letters at once, mixing the vibrations.

Physical		Emotional		Spiritual	
J	10/1	W	23/5	L	12/3
O	15/6	I	9	E	5
H	8	N	14/5	N	14/5
N	14/5	S	19/1	N	14/5
		T	20/2	O	15/6
		O	15/6	N	14/5
		N	14/5		

In the Transit column, you'll see *OWL* on line 2 and if you read down the list, it's a running list of the letters in the name. Above you'll see

J 10/1
O 15/6
H 8
N 14/5, etc.

and the letters are listed like that in this column. One *J*, 6 *O*s, 8 *H*s and 5 *N*s are in the "John" column. In the *W* column, the letters are listed for as many years as there are numerical values, so *W* appears 5 times, *I* appears 9 times, *N* appears 5 times, etc.

5. Add the passing letters to determine the Personal Motivation for the year ($O \ W \ L = 6 + 5 + 3 = 14/5$).

6. Add the day and month of birth, and the passing year, to determine the Personal Year for the Life Path ($10 + 9 + 1941 = 16 = 7$ in the Personal Year column for 1941 in Table 9).

Let me emphasize once again: the name that matters for the Life Path graph is always the original, full and first one. Let's look at John Winston Lennon's chart, shown in Table 9 on pages 100–101.

Lennon's personal life was well documented, which makes it easier to analyze the graph.

Between age 1 and 2, the conjunction of 14 and 16 suggested a structural problem in the family (Path 24/6). A while after that, his parents separated. More or less when he was 3, the conjunction of 16 and 18 was kind of tough for a small kid. And around age 5 and 6, the two number 2s represented weakness and vulnerability: around that time, John's father, who eventually abandoned him, wanted to take him to New Zealand, where he was living at the time. Still, John preferred to stay with his uncles. Ultimately the father left John with the mother, and John's mother gave him back to the uncles. The conjunction of 22, between age 7 and 8, indicates great insight, some kind of illumination, or a big and painful obstacle.

Between ages 14 and 19, the conjunction of three *N*s indicates sudden happenings, abrupt ends, shock, fast changes, movement, and locomotion. That conjunction meets Essence 16 and Personal Year 24 at age 18, suggesting a heavier environment. That was the time of his mother's death, an event that was most relevant to his formation as an artist and as a man. Obviously, this does not imply that every *NN* conjunction will necessarily anticipate the same situation for other people. There are many ways we can interpret symbols, but the characteristics mentioned earlier about *N* conjunctions underline a very influential event in one's life.

In 1960, the letter *T* symbolizes marriage, and *J* stands for responsibilities. In 1961, the conjunction of *O*s indicates duty, emotional trouble, while *T* kept the marriage symbolism. There was a conjunction of 14 and 18, which denotes a marriage in the dark, for 14 is the number of "the art," the conjunction of polarities, and 18 explains the source and direction of such a union—stepping on eggs in the dark. That was the scenario when John's girlfriend, Cynthia, found herself pregnant. Note also that 18 may indicate an unexpected pregnancy, as well as an abortion. They married on February 23, 1962, and even though it was not an unhappy marriage, it was not a happy one either. Lennon said in interviews that he and Cynthia never had anything to tell to each other.

Until October 1967, approximately, the conjunction grew stronger and then weaker, reflecting the ups and downs of the unpleasantness that the couple was facing. Nevertheless, between 1967 and 1968, the letter *O* was not conjunct with another one anymore, which changes the vibration completely. When a letter conjuncts with another of the same kind, it is a sign of a saturated vibration, one ready to explode—or implode. Thus, the connotation of only one letter *O* turns to a happy meeting, a love affair, and things like that—the other side of the exaggeration.

In May 1968, John and Yoko spent their first night together, and recorded their first album, *Unfinished Music Number 1: Two Virgins*. Between October 1968 and October 1969 one more conjunction related to death, accidents, and similar activities took place (in July 1969), when John, Yoko, and their sons, Julian and Kyoko, were involved in a car crash in Scotland, caused by John's myopic lack of vision. The same conjunction of 16 and 19 appears again around age 31/32. I do not know if that one materialized, but it was probably diluted, since there is no reference to any related event in his life near that time.

Between 1973 and 1978 there was a *W* in the emotional column, which tends to describe the beginning and/or the ending of an affair. Exactly when the transit of the letter starts, in October 1973, John and Yoko separated for eighteen months, a period when John dated his assistant, May Pang. In the last months of 1976, there was a conjunction of number 6 indicating the same thing that an *OO* conjunction would—trouble in matters relating to love. But the rule that says that a conjunction may barely materialize itself every time it comes in the graph may apply here; for John used to declare that the period of raising Sean was the happiest of his life. The third and last letter *N* conjunction came between 1975 and 1980, ending two months before the murder. It looks dilu-ted, and it is interesting to notice that John's death did not appear in any of the divinatory systems that Yoko used to use then.

The only sign of the impending murder was that she had an intuition, and asked John to travel, as she had done before. She insisted that he go with Sean to Bermuda, and he refused. Yoko declared that she only understood that after the tragedy. I assume that not *everything* must be in the numbers—I mean, not every-thing is supposed to be understandable for the interpreter. There are some tunes the numbers whisper that we cannot hear, for no matter how large one's mind is, it will not be able to apprehend the infinite—because if one apprehends the infinite, then the infi-nite is no more. In the same way a dog is able to listen to some sounds that we humans cannot, maybe it is not a human condi-tion to have absolute knowledge about infinity. Every mind, and even every being, is a universe with its own laws, principles, and mechanisms.

Table 10 (pages 104–105), and Table 11 (pages 106–109) will help you decipher the meanings of the conjunctions of both let-ters and numbers.

TABLE **10.** THE MEANING OF LETTERS IN THE LIFE GRAPH.

A Beginning, renovation, activity, direction, command, power, shine. *Conjunction:* Virus, stress, too much yang energy.

B Union, society, division, rupture, sensibility, slowness. *Conjunction:* Excessive sensibility, separation, accidents, depression, apathy.

C Friends, creativity, new things, new people, fun, happiness. *Conjunction:* Creativity and anxiety, dissipation, dilution.

D Rationality, work, waiting, patience, rigor, method. *Conjunction:* Limits, tension, repression, hypocrisy, frustration, traditionalism, immobility, stopping.

E Movement, moving, changing, renovation, sex, new experiences, adventure. *Conjunction:* Nervous problems, drug excess, sexual excess, urological or gynecological problems, big chance—for better or worse—a definitive one.

F Affection, family, emotion, responsibility, harmony, stability. *Conjunction:* Emotion, passion, ecstasy and love—but all that uncontrolled in a destructive/repressive way.

G Slowness, isolation, reflection, meditation, religion. *Conjunction:* Fakes, betrayal, feeling of being observed, mystery, apprehension, religious fraud.

H Rationality, business, money, justice, law, prosperity. *Conjunction:* Tension, oppression, business chance for the quick ones.

I Agitation, anxiety, activity, groups, travel, evolution, growing up. *Conjunction:* Emotional trouble, rise of hidden situations, humanitarianism.

J Beginning again, recovering power, experience, command, a turning point. *Conjunction:* Excessive responsibilities, tension, overactivity.

K Unconventional, intuition, duality, discovering, intriguing experiences, renovation. *Conjunction:* Misunderstanding, mistake, insecurity, depression, revelation, great psychic power, capacity for managing trouble.

L Wisdom, knowledge, acquired happiness. A rush may be a fatal error. *Conjunction:* Waste of energy, victimization, anxiety.

M Sudden transformation, work efforts, results, death (symbolic or material). *Conjunction:* Too much work, radical change, depth, death (of any kind).

TABLE 10. THE MEANING OF LETTERS IN THE LIFE GRAPH. (CONT.)

N Change, travel, pleasure, adventure, quickness, originality, indolence, laziness. *Conjunction:* Accidents, distraction, risking life due to impulsiveness or inconsequence.

O Passion, love affair, sons, family, impulse, romance, partiality. *Conjunction:* Cardiac diseases, blind passion, explosion, jealousy, aggressive instincts.

P Rupture, fall, isolation, introspection, changing of aim and destiny, block, impediment, spirituality. *Conjunction:* Isolation, lack of contact, prolonged disease, forced reflection.

Q Money, gain, heritage, prize, recompense, hope. *Conjunction:* Prosperity, but hope in excess can generate negligence, and therefore, injury.

R Nervousness, asperity, aggressiveness, concern, longing, agility, confusion. *Conjunction:* Accidents, drugs, illusion, delusion, intoxication, fraud, mistake, danger, dissimulation.

S Great force, pretension, ambition, ego, fights, physical activity, capacity. *Conjunction:* Depression, loneliness, lack of power.

T Couples, partners, recovered conscience, self-criticism, society, weirdness, uncommon, transcendence. *Conjunction:* Guilt, troubled by conscience, victimization, haunting.

U Plenitude, expansion, amplitude, megalomania, boredom. *Conjunction:* End of a cycle, lose and gain, ups and downs, instability.

V Giving, charity, work, ambition, development. *Conjunction:* Annulment of the ego, blind ambition, hurting, losses.

W Changes, transformation, adventures, boldness, fun, travel. *Conjunction:* Sudden changes, surprises, unpredictable happenings, good news.

X Possessiveness, suffocating relationship, jealousy, a possum. *Conjunction:* Unhappiness coming from distorted point of view.

Y Paternity, maternity, friendship, intuition, intellectuality, division, duality, conflict, introspection. *Conjunction:* Trouble with sons, drugs, heavy conscience, problematic spirituality.

Z All or nothing in terms of money, material possessions, and justice. Health problems can be solved with logic. *Conjunction:* Depression, tension, platonic passion, death, suffering can be avoided using logic.

TABLE 11. NUMERICAL CONJUNCTIONS.

NUMBER	CHARACTERISTICS
1/1	Inutile (useless) super-activity, fight for power, excesses in general, authoritarianism, inflexibility.
1/2	A conflict of interests, but also complementary opposites.
1/3	Harmony, accord, success, practicality, creativity.
1/4	Dissonance between speed and slowness, but if the relationship is established as a conductor and the conducted, there will be harmony.
1/5	Realization, dynamism, mutability.
1/6	Harmony coming from an acceptance of responsibilities, indicates some conflict between logic and ambition.
1/7	Euphoria, gradual change, rationality. The numbers are complementary, regardless of the fact that 1 is too hurried for the methodical 7.
1/8	Complementary vibrations, accomplished power, hard battle, rivalry.
1/9	Tension, controlled and channeled anxiety can produce creativity, cooperation, and balance.
1/11	Great force, charisma, development, rivalry, there may be cooperation if the ego does not prevail.
1/22	A growing up, intelligence, leadership, generosity.
2/2	Fragility, great sensibility, even passivity, cowardly, inoperative, inertia.
2/3	Some compatibility, even though 2 is too slow for 3's haste.
2/4	Slowness, stability. Slow but safe evolution.
2/5	Sensuality, passion, complementary, should make sure that one doesn't end up being a slave to his or her personal desires.
2/6	Kindness, communication, harmony, but not practical.

TABLE 11. NUMERICAL CONJUNCTIONS. (CONT.)

NUMBER	CHARACTERISTICS
2/7	Mysticism, research, psychic, subtlety, serenity.
2/8	Balance between ambition and emotion.
2/9	Exaggerated emotionalism, lack of control.
2/22	Great potential, psychic energy, humanitarian relationship, passivity.
3/3	Great imagination, but small realization.
3/4	Realization and imagination, ideas being mate-rialized.
3/5	Accord, vivacity, youth, enthusiasm.
3/6	Harmony, kindness, equilibrium, comfort.
3/7	Divided between social conviviality and meditative introspection.
3/8	Practicality and creativity, realization, work, credibility.
3/9	Vivacity, expression, dynamism, balance.
3/11	Excitation, boldness, open to knowledge, perception, great turning.
3/22	Influential friends, favors, gain.
4/4	Many things to do, a lack of imagination, sterility, effort, tension, repression, lack of ambition and motivation.
4/5	Conflict of interests conducive to growing up, frontal shock.
4/6	Practicality and kindness combined, stability, understanding.
4/7	Reasonable, stable, bad humor, sullenness, avarice.
4/8	Dryness, rigidity, materialism, good business.
4/9	Reason and compassion, limitation and expansion.
4/11	Divergent vibrations, but only 4 can put 11 on a more objective path, while 11 may amplify 4's dullness. Communication may be difficult between these numbers.

TABLE 11. NUMERICAL CONJUNCTIONS. (CONT.)

NUMBER	CHARACTERISTICS
4/22	The instructed and the instructor, a complementary and harmonized combination.
5/5	Abuse of freedom, impulsiveness, volubility, learning from adventures and risks taken.
5/6	Divergent natures, shock, lack of understanding, ups and downs, and unfaithfulness.
5/7	Fearlessness, philosophic analysis, theory and practice, some confusion.
5/8	Impulsiveness and rationalism, attraction between opposites.
5/9	Convergent energies, positive changing, balance, success.
5/11	Great originality and daring, sometimes petulance.
5/22	Boldness, evolution, progress, spiritual taming.
6/6	Too much emotionalism, vulnerability, delays, something related to the family.
6/7	Loneliness even when not alone, mind versus heart.
6/8	Repression, fear, insecurity, matter versus emotion.
6/9	Creativity, balance, objective, activity.
6/11	Difficult communication.
6/22	Giving, charity, love, public service.
7/7	Intelligence, depth, slowness, criticism, bad humor, cerebral tension.

TABLE 11. NUMERICAL CONJUNCTIONS. (CONT.)

NUMBER	CHARACTERISTICS
7/8	Dichotomy, Manicheanism, realization.
7/9	Inconstancy, unpredictability.
7/11	Great spiritual potential, philosophic, intellectual, little concern for convention, isolation in society.
7/22	Head in the sky, feet on the ground.
8/8	Tension, self-destruction,. productivity, materialism, greed, legal problems.
8/9	Balance between matter and spirit.
8/11	Capacity to be unconventional without shocking, complementary.
8/22	A perfect accord, richness, great change, opportunity.
9/9	Excessive energy, difficult communication, speed, velocity, accidents, tension.
9/11	Perception, evolution, growing up, breaking conventions, revolutionary.
9/22	Politics, group, party, religion, transcendence or foolishness.
11/11	Illumination or craziness, transcendence or degradation.
11/22	Complementary, intuition, objectivity, assimilation.
22/22	All or nothing.

PERSONAL YEARS AND MONTHS

As you already know, the Personal Year represents the kind of vibration that rules a certain year, a period that runs from one birthday to the next, not from January 1st to December 31st—unless, of course, you were born on one of these dates! It is very helpful and important to know your Personal Year in conjunction with your Personal Month, for it gives a very accurate analysis.

The calculation is quite simple: for the Personal Year, add the day and month of birth to the year you want to know about. For your Personal Month, add the Personal Year to the month you want to know about. The same recommendations about conjunctions between numbers apply to the months and year, as long as you remember that the year is more important than the month, and the yearly vibration will carry more "weight" than the one for the month.

Say you were born on June 15, 1975, and you want to know what 2005 will be like. To set your Personal Year number you add 2005 + 6 + 15 to get 2026, and 2 + 0 + 2 + 6 to get 10, and then 1 + 0 to get 1. We never add numbers one by one, but actually take the numbers of year, month, and day separately, to get the correct result. As you see, the origin of this number 1 is not 19, or 28, but 10. Also, fourfold numbers such as 2026 contain additional meanings.[36]

After exploring number 1 in Table 12 (pages 112–114), you can learn how August of 2005 will be by adding 2026 (the Personal Year number) to 8 (the number for August). You will find the number 2034/9 (2 + 0 + 3 + 4 = 9), your Personal Month number for August for August 2005. Look 9 up in Table 12 (page 114). In this way, you can be prepared to deal with situations arising from the vibrations of these two numbers.

---

36. My next book, *The Book of Numbers*, due to publish in the spring of 2002, will explain these meanings in detail.

The table suggests that 2005 is a year of new beginnings for you. And August is a very important month, because you'll know where you have missed the mark and if your plans are on the right track. August won't be an easy month, but if you have set the stage well, you should have some nice things happening to you—not by chance, but because of the hard work you have already done to prepare for this time period.

TABLE 12. PERSONAL YEARS AND MONTHS.

1—Time to begin things in the right way, recommendable for every activity of leadership. Independence. Time for growing up and being ambitious. The very moment to start everything you want to see fructifying later. Must be active, define objectives, and not let other people deal with your job and your things. It is not the time to count on any kind of outside help; things will only succeed if you do yourself what you must do. Follow your own opinion, but be careful not to be too arrogant.

2—Gestation period. Wait. One must let things happen naturally, not being pushy, not trying to be in command all the time. Patience is a must. Resist the temptation of being too exposed. It is normal to feel fragile and vulnerable during this year or month, because of this number's exacerbated sensibility. How-ever, it is common to have a very good love affair, or even friendship, in such a period. One must try not to be too much dependent on other people.

3—Generally, it is a positive period, when the investments of **Personal Year or Month 1** may start to fructify. The energy is full of fun, feasts, optimism, happiness, but be careful not to distract yourself too much and forget the things you have to do. You must express yourself. Make your aims and intentions public. Be careful not to say too much to the wrong person. This is an especially good period for artists and children.

4—Organization, work, limits, restrictions. Some people consider this period kind of boring, for it is the time to establish the things you started in **Personal Month/Year 1**. You should expect to do lots of things, not all of them exactly pleasant, but all necessary. There is always a moment to put the house in order, to deal with documents, papers, and bureaucracy; to work hard, to get exhausted—but after all, you will be constructing something. It is a good test of your will, patience, and your determination. Things tend to go slowly, but the conquests will probably be definitive or stable ones.

5—Changes, instability, experimentation. This is the moment for alterations in plans, for changing the way. Good for resting a little after the busy period before. It is good to let yourself feel unattached when living under the edge of 5. The libido and sex-uality are pulsing a lot, as if adolescence is coming back, making you ready for any nutty adventure—which may be good. Travels are a must, as well as moving and changing in general. Try not to be futile or superficial. Try to avoid an

TABLE 12. PERSONAL YEARS AND MONTHS. (CONT.)

excess of drugs and food, and do not confuse unattachment with inconsequence. Go with the flow, don't worry about destiny, just go. The worst in this period is to stay, for 5 only exists through motion.

6—Harmony, peace, tranquillity, rest (emotionally speaking). Love, passion, family affairs, marriage, birth. You should accept the responsibilities that are typical of the number, but only accept your own and not other people's responsibilities. Do not overwhelm yourself trying to fix the world. Good for buying a house or (re)constructing a home. Try not to get into someone else's business; you may have a problem if you do. Do not be invasive or jealous. Try to conciliate as much as you can. Good period for arts and artists.

7—Reflection, meditation, research, spirituality. It is natural that you feel the need to be alone, away from agitation. Great possibilities for self-knowledge, but only if you are not afraid of seeing your own full reflection in the mirror, containing both your angelic and your demonic side. Tendency to melancholy, sadness, depression, but it can all be avoided if you close yourself and stay balanced. Excellent for research and study; the intellect works particularly well during this period, with great capacity for assimilation. If you are a skeptical and cynical person, you will find these characteristics amplified during the transit of 7. A chronic health problem tends to be stronger during this period, so it's time for a check-up. Try not to invest too much in money matters, be prudent and reserved. Do not take unnecessary risks. Try not to be cranky. Above all, behold, because learning is the best part of 7.

8—All or nothing, especially about money, material possessions and laws. If you have something going on regarding justice, the solution may come during this period. But don't think it will necessarily be a good one; it depends on previous facts in the chart and in the whole process, with its particularities. Good for investments, for expanding business, but count more on rationality than on intuition—8 is like a hole that attracts dense thoughts, thus intuition may contaminate. Be calm. Too much speed can ruin everything. Wait for lots of work, be dynamic, and be ready for getting back all the good and bad things you've done before, for this is the period of karma.

TABLE 12. PERSONAL YEARS AND MONTHS. (CONT.)

9—End, closing, everything that began in the 1 period is supposed to end here—not in the death sense, but in the sense of closing a cycle. Agitation, impatience, and anguish are common this period, and can be the combustibles for great realization. On the other hand, one must avoid channeling one's stress to others, which would be unfair. Excellent for travels and moving, as good as 5. One must try not to lose emotional control. Reflect about the last 9 years and project the next ones.

11—When everything hidden (the occult) emerges. Inspiration, intuition. It is common that the uncommon turns into common now. Since it comes after a **Year/Month 1**, it is a substitute for 2, and it happens to be a double 1, stronger and special. The tendency is to act outside of any rule, even your own rules. It's okay to be radical, but one should really know what one is doing, otherwise one may be controlled by hidden energies. Occultism, magick, and religion.

22—Everything gets bigger and out of proportion. Tends to a certain megalomania, even though it is a moment of great realization. Good discernment is a must for you to retain a balance between an unreal dream and a will that you must put in practice. This is the moment of the Great Work.

FINAL CONSIDERATIONS

Now that you have the entire basis for calculating your own chart, remember: whenever you are going to interpret it for yourself or for another, be critical but not self-punitive, and always be as impartial as you can. A good thing for you is not necessarily good for another. Let the chart itself show you the way, don't judge or preconceive things.

I hope your initiation to the numbers will be a productive experience for you!

BIBLIOGRAPHY

Bhagavad-Gita. There are many translations of this book available. *The Bhagavad-Gita*, Antonio de Nicolás, trans. York Beach, ME: Nicolas-Hays, 1990 has been used in this volume.

The New English Bible with Apocrypha. New York: Oxford University Press. 1971

Blanchefort, Jean de. *Guia da Magia.* São Paulo: Maltese, 1992.

Blavatsky, Helena. *The Voice of Silence.* Santa Barbara, CA: Concord Grove, 1989.

Budge, E. A. Wallis. *Egyptian Magic.* London: Routledge & Kegan Paul, 1899; Reprinted New York: Dover, 1971.

Camaisar, Rosabis, trans. *O Caibalion.* São Paulo: Pensamento, 1978.

Cavendish, Richard, ed. *Encyclopedia of the Unexplained.* New York: Viking/Penguin, 1990.

Chaboche, François-Xavier. *Vida e Mistério dos Números.* São Paulo: Hemus, 1979.

Cissay, Monique. *Numerologia: A Importância do Nome no Seu Destino.* São Paulo: Pensamento, 1984.

Crowley, Aleister. *The Book of Thoth.* York Beach, ME: Samuel Weiser, 1969.

———. *The Law is for All.* Phoenix, AZ: New Falcon, 1993.

Dethlefsen, Thorwald. *Challenge of Fate: Ancient Wisdom as the Path to Human Wholeness.* London: Coventure, 1984.

Dickerman, Alexandra Collins. *Following Your Path: Using Myths, Symbols, and Images.* Los Angeles: J. P. Tarcher, 1992.

Dodge, Ellin & Carol Ann Schuler. *The Vibes Book.* New York: Samuel Weiser, 1979.

Editors of Rolling Stone. *The Ballad of John & Yoko.* New York: Rolling Stone, 1981.

Fortune, Dion. *Applied Magic*. York Beach, ME: Samuel Weiser, 1969; 2000.

——. *The Mystical Qabalah*. York Beach, ME: Samuel Weiser, 1984; revised edition, 2000.

Hitchcock, Helyn. *Helping Yourself with Numerology*. New York: Parker Publishing, 1988.

Javane, Faith and Dusty Bunker. *Numerology and the Divine Triangle*. Atglen, PA: Whitford Press, 1979.

Koltuv, Barbara Black. *The Book of Lilith*. York Beach, ME: Nicolas-Hays, 1986.

Lao Tzu. *The Tao Te Ching*. There are many versions and translations of this book available. We have used *Lao Tzu: Tao Te Ching*, John C. H. Wu, trans., Paul K. T. Sih, ed. New York: St. John's University Press, 1961; *Lao Tsu: Tao Te Ching*, Gia-Fu Feng and Jane English, trans. London: Wildwood House, 1973; and *Lao Tzu: Tao Te Ching*, Ch'u Ta-Kao, trans. London: Allen & Unwin, 1937.

Levi, Eliphas. *The Great Secret*. France, 1861. York Beach, ME: Samuel Weiser, 1976, 2000.

——. *History of Magic*. France, 1913. York Beach, ME: Samuel Weiser, 1970, 1999.

——. *Key of the Mysteries*. London: Rider, 1959; New York: Samuel Weiser, 1971.

——. *Transcendental Magic*. York Beach, ME: Samuel Weiser, 1968.

Lewis, Ralph M. *Behold the Sign: Ancient Symbolism*. San Jose, CA: A.M.O.R.C., 1944.

Lorenz, Francisco Valdomiro. *Cabala: A Tradição Esotérica de Ocidente*. São Paulo: Pensamento, 1912.

Louvigny, Philippe de. *Guia Completo de Numerologia*. Lisboa: Edições 70, 1991.

Malagolli, Marco Antonio. *John Lennon*. São Paulo: Editora Três, 1981.

Phelps, Ruth. *The Universe of Numbers*. San Jose, CA: A.M.O.R.C. 1984.

Piobb, P.-V. *Formulário de Alta Magia*. Rio de Janeiro: Francisco Alves Editora, 1982.

Sabellicus, Jorg. *A Magia dos Números.* Lisboa: Edições 70, 1986.

Westcott, W. Wynn. *Numbers: Their Occult Power and Mystic Virtues.* London: Theosophical Publishing Society, 1902. Published in English in a multi-volume work called *The Collectanea Hermetica* by Samuel Weiser, York Beach, ME: 1988.

Ziegler, Gerd. *Tarot—Mirror of the Soul.* York Beach, ME: Samuel Weiser, 1988.

INDEX

(Numbers in bold indicate pages where definitions are given)

Abrasax, 33
Adam, first wife of, 51
Adonai, 58
AIN, 58
alchemy, 40
alphabets
    Greek, 24
    Hebrew, 24, 34, 53
androgynous symbolism, 50
Apocalypse, 53
arcana number, 91
archetypal energy, 17
archetypes, 18, 21
    qabalistic, 22

Baal, Astarte, and Melkart, 34
balance number, 72
basic challenge number, 83
basic credit numbers, 83
birth, date of, 18
Brahma, Vishu, and Shiva, 34

cardinal points, 37
Chaboche, François-Xavier, 29,
    51
choice number, 70
color
    blue, 35
    red, 41
communicability, 35
communication, 43
creation, 44

creativity, 35
Crowley, Aleister, 32, 38, 50, 92
cube of 6, 43
cycles, 85

death, 38
    of a soul, 38
de Gerase, Nicomano, 29
Demonic Sephiroth, 51
de Seville, Isidoro, 53
destiny, 65
destruction, 45
dharma number 73
divine manifestations, 48
duality, 31

8, 14, 46
elements, 37
    air, 35
11, 14, 50
Elohim, 40
energy, psychic, 56
enlightenment, 20
esoteric
    challenge, 67
    interpretation, 66
    number, 67
essence number, 71
essential states, 37
exoteric
    challenge, 68
    number, 67

Father, Son and Holy Spirit, 34
feet, 37
female insubordination, 51
fire element, 30
first challenge number, 83
5, 14, 38
formation of personality number, 76
Fortune, Dion, 51
foundation number, 74
4, 13, 20, 36
frustration, 38

general challenge number, 69
Great Mother, 51

Harris, Frieda, 92
health, 46
heart number, 75
heredity number, 78
Hermes Trismegistos, 32, 34
Holy Guardian Angel, 58

initiation, 20
intuition, 32, 56
intuitive process, 59

karma number, 74
karmic challenge number, 84
Koltuv, Barbara Black, 51

Lao Tzu, 28, 33, 36
laziness, 38
legs, 37
Lennon, John, 65
    name graphic of, 77
    personal year, 86
letters
    in life graph, meaning of, 104–105

and number equivalents, 24
and numbers, conjunction of, 98
Levi, Eliphas, 52
life path number, 98
Lilith, 51

magic square, 55
magick, 60
major arcana, 53
Malagolli, Marco Antonio, 68
Masons, 51
mental illness, 20
metaphysical power, 17
minor arcana, 95
mobius strip, 46
money, 46
months, personal, 111
Moon, 30
mysterium conjunctionis, 33
mysticism, 56

name graphic, 76
9, 14, 48
nonexistence, 27
Nuit, 47, 50
numbers
    basic, 13, 21
    composed, 20, 21, 54
    diabolical, 32
    elementary, 18
    essence of, 19
    even, 18
    and major arcana in Thoth Deck, 93
    master, 13, 19, 53
    odd, 18
    odd and even, 18
    perfect, 30
    personal year, 85, 86
    and profession, 80

and sex, 82
spiral projection of, 22
symbolism, 92
numerical conjunctions,
    106–109
numerological chart, 65
numerology, 17

Oddin, Frega, and Thor, 34
1, 13, 20, 28
opposites
    equilibrium between, 40
    union between, 34
organization, 36
Ormuzd, Ahriman, and
    Mithra, 34
Osiris, Isis, and Horus, 34

Pandora's box, 49
passion, 62
Path
    of Abrasax, 53
    of the lamb, 53
path of destiny number, 69
pentagram, 40
perfection, 42
personal
    month, 110
    year, 110
personality
    manifestation of, 18
    numbers, formation of, 76
pessimism, 38
Phelps, Ruth, 32, 33, 34, 37
Philon, 33
pinnacles, 85, 87
    1st, 87
    2nd, 88
    3rd, 88
    4th, 88
Piobb, P.-V., 55

polarity, 17
positions, Yang, Yin and neu-
    tral, 19
potential, 27
power, 28
power of will number, 75
procreation, 40
professional advice number,
    79
Prometheus, myth of, 31
Pythagoras, 17, 19
Pythagoreans, 43, 44, 51, 54

Qabalah, 24
Qabalistic
    Paths, 32, 41
    worlds, 37
Qliphoth, 51

regeneration, 61

Sabellicus, Jorg, 30, 50, 54
Sacred Unity, 32
Saturn, 86
seasons, 37
second challenge number, 83
second cycle number, 86
second name number, 79
7, 14, 44
sex, 39
sexuality, 56, 57
sexuality number, 81
Shiva, 45
6, 14, 42
solar energy, 28
stress number, 72
subconcious number, 78
Sun, 92
Sun, Moon and Earth, 34
synthesis, 34
synthesis number, 68

tarot, 13
    deck, choosing one, 92
    21st arcana of, 35
temper, 34, 37
tetractys, 29, 30
Thelema, 40
third cycle number, 87
Thoth Tarot, 92
    numbers and major arcana
        in, 93
3, 13, 20
traditionalism, 42
transformation, 38
    of essential archetypes, 48
tree of life, 35

triangular combination, 19
Triple Trinity, 49
Trismegistos, 37
29, 11, 19
22, 14, 52
2, 13, 31

water element, 33
Westcott, W. Wynn, 29, 34, 37,
    43, 47, 58

years, personal, 111

0, 13, 27
Zeus, 31

ABOUT THE AUTHOR

Johann Heyss is a writer and musician who lives in Rio de Janeiro, Brazil. Since his adolescence he has been researching various paths of esoteric study. His interest in the numbers' archetypes prompted him to look beyond popular methods, and his new system combines many traditions. He encourages people to read their own numbers and teaches his interpretive technique in workshops and private classes. Heyss continues to work as a singer/composer. He has performed in many Brazilian states, as well as in New York City, where he lived during 1998. He has produced two CDs, *Look Carefully* and AL A.H.A. He welcomes correspondence from readers in English and Portuguese at heyss@yahoo.com, or write to him in care of the publisher.